D0525458

VARIATIONS ON A THEME

Some guidelines for everyday
Christians who want to reform
the Liturgy

Michael H. Taylor

1973

GALLIARD

LONDON: STAINER AND BELL LTD

SBN 85249 172 7 (Paperback)
 85249 283 9 (Hardback)

Galliard (Printers) Ltd, Queen Anne's Road, Great Yarmouth, Norfolk
Printed in England

CONTENTS

PREFACE

Large numbers of our contemporaries have ceased to involve themselves in Christian worship at least as we have usually thought of it, and what follows is in no way an appeal to them to change their minds. I doubt that people can be reasoned into worship anymore than they can be argued into faith. Amongst those who remain in our congregations the more restive show a good deal of interest in new ways of worshipping and a readiness to experiment. Whilst hoping to be regarded as their ally, it has not been my intention to offer them another collection of suggestions and ideas. These do not seem to me to be in short supply. What people appear to lack more often is a framework of understanding which enables them to give less than superficial reasons for what is done. It is one such framework that I have tried to provide within a reasonably limited compass, making reference to history, theology and practice where this seemed appropriate.

I have operated as a 'middle-man', drawing on the insights and learning of others to whom I have nothing to offer in return but my gratitude. What I have learnt from them I have attempted to set down in a straightforward way, bearing in mind the needs of a number of students known to me, and those everyday members of the church and its ministry who are expected to take responsibility for its worship—or would very much like to do so!

No doubt our writing and thinking on this subject reveal a self-consciousness which will vanish like smoke when confidence returns; and no one pretends of course that new forms, however well thought out, can give new life, any more than new wine-skins can of themselves produce new wine. But it is not the whole of our vocation to sit back and wait for God, and we are advised on good authority that when new wine becomes available it is fresh skins and not old ones that make the more satisfactory containers.

I am grateful to Faber & Faber Ltd. and Harcourt, Brace, Jovanovich Inc. for permission to quote some lines from T. S. Eliot's *Four Quartets*, and to a number of friends for their practical help.

v

Michael H. Taylor
Northern Baptist College
Manchester
July 1973

I

THEME

Christian worship presents us with a landscape of almost bewildering variety, and if we are to find our way it will be wise to begin with a few fairly basic directions. It is only when we know the road that we grow more confident and gain a certain freedom to enjoy the scenery. These directions can be conveniently organised under the following four headings:

1 Many services, one Liturgy
2 Bare bones
3 Telling the Story
4 The status quo

Many services, one Liturgy

The whole of life can be regarded as an act of worship, but in this discussion we are mainly concerned with the more organised occasions we usually refer to as services. It would not be difficult to compile a fairly considerable list. Some, like weddings and funerals, baptisms, confirmations and ordinations have to do with special events. Others are part of the more normal and on-going pattern of life. For example, earlier generations of Anglicans were familiar with Morning and Evening Prayer, not on weekdays when these were said mostly by the clergy, but certainly at week-ends when until comparatively recently they were the main item on the Sunday programme. The Free Churches on the other hand traditionally held a devotional meeting for prayer and Bible study during the week, and in some places still do. It was referred to as the mid-week service. On Sundays their preaching service includes hymns and prayers and readings but tends to find its centre of interest in the sermon.

Two other examples may be mentioned of a rather different kind. One is the occasion which is specifically designed to present the Christian message to the unbeliever in the hope that he will respond to the Gospel and be converted. It can take the form of a mass rally. Once upon a time it was the idea behind the Sunday evening service which was intended for 'sinners' whereas the morning was for 'saints'! The other example is the service based on a theme like race relations or some other issue arising out of the contemporary scene. The theme is presented in an imaginative way using visual aids, dialogue, discussions, appropriate songs, readings and prayers. The congregation is informed about the issue itself, helped to see it in the light of the Christian faith, and challenged to make a response.

We tend to make only hazy distinctions between all these services, failing to recognise a number of important differences. Morning and Evening Prayer, or Mattins and Evensong, are not simply two more services among the rest. They are distinctive in being part of a daily discipline of prayer and devotion known as the Daily Office or, more technically, as the Canonical Hours. Its origin is not entirely clear. It was no doubt partly inspired by the old Jewish hours of prayer mentioned in the Bible (Daniel 6.10, Acts 2.15, 10.9, 3.1) which were not unrelated to the hours of sacrifice in the Temple and the arrangements in the synagogues. At a later date devout Christians wished to add to these and, not surprisingly, their times for prayer corresponded with the Roman divisions of the day. When Jewish and Roman time-tables were put together the result was a round the clock discipline beginning with Vigils at 2 a.m., followed by Lauds at daybreak, Prime in the early morning, Terce at 9 a.m., Sext at noon, None at 3 p.m., Vespers at 6 p.m. and Compline, which is still used, at 8 p.m. These services found a natural home in the life of the monastic communities though much of the material either was reminiscent of or gradually emerged into the more public worship of the church. During the Middle Ages they became largely the concern of the clergy and by the time of the Reformation were said in two groups, one in the morning and the other in the evening. In the sixteenth century Archbishop Cranmer combined his own skills with these older traditions to create the Mattins and Evensong of the English prayer book. When these became the main Sunday services in many Anglican churches and the only services of the week for the majority of churchgoers, their distinctive character was obscured. They were no longer understood as part of an everyday routine.

Some of the other services, although no one could deny that they are in a sense acts of worship, might be better called by another name, since they have a different purpose. Preaching the Gospel to unbelievers is Christian propaganda or evangelism to which all and sundry may be invited. It is not the worship of Christian people from which the unbeliever has often been carefully excluded by the

2

church. It may not be wise to invite him before he is adequately prepared. The service based upon a theme may again have a real element of worship, but it is often more strictly concerned with education and the enlightening and quickening of the Christian conscience.

There are then many services, but it is important to distinguish them from each other and from one service in particular. It is referred to by a number of titles, and some of them have the disadvantage of being heavy with associations which quickly arouse prejudice and hinder rather than help. In some circles it is known as the Mass, in others as the Eucharist (a Greek work for thanksgiving) or Holy Communion, in others as the Lord's Supper. For want of a better idea we shall have to use the most neutral word I can think of and that is the *Liturgy*, though even that provokes negative reactions and conjures up unwelcome pictures of stereotyped and elaborate rituals. It is a word that has been in more popular use in the Eastern Orthodox part of the church than in the West. It comes from the Greek language. We do not wish to build too much on its meaning, but roughly speaking to perform a liturgy was to perform a service and not necessarily a religious one at that. It will serve as a convenient way of distinguishing one organised act of worship from all the rest as indeed Orthodox Christians here tended to do for a very long time. There are many services but one Liturgy.

By singling it out we do not suggest that the others do not have an entirely proper place. No-one questions that private devotion, a regular discipline of prayer, evangelistic rallies, devotional meetings, educational programmes are not valid and important aspects of the life of the church. What is being suggested is that the Liturgy has a unique and central place. It is an opinion which has become more and more widely shared in recent times. A study of the story of the church during 2,000 years reveals that it has often been shared before and leads us to the conclusion that here above all is the distinctive act of Christian worship. One movement in Britain which has done much to help us to recover this insight is Parish and People, and perhaps we may be allowed to quote from the report of their conference in 1962. Their name for the Liturgy is Parish Communion and

"By 'the Parish Communion' is meant the celebration of the Holy Eucharist, with the communion of the people (i.e. everybody sharing in the bread and wine),

3

in a parish church as the chief service of the day, or, better, as the assembly of the Christian community for the worship of God; for even the phrase 'the chief service of the day' is unsatisfactory if it is understood to mean *a* service—one among several—and not *the* service—the divine Liturgy." (p. 6)

Here then is the first clear instruction this guide would wish to give. Amongst all the variety, look out for the one service which is in a class by itself. If we recognise it we may find our way better elsewhere. It may help in deciding what is essential and what is not. It may help in discussions about an appropriate pattern for Sunday activities if traditional arguments for getting together regularly on that day remain sound. We must of course respect the insights of Quakers and other groups which lead them to disapprove of all this talk about the Liturgy, but where it is accepted as the characteristic thing for Christians to do and as the one fixed point, it will help us to enter into a greater freedom to do a variety of different things at other times or maybe to do nothing else at all.

But to insist that the Liturgy is Christian worship par excellence does little to tell us why or to explain exactly what it is. More directions are needed.

Bare bones

Even when we have confined our discussion, at least for the time being, to the central and distinctive act of Christian worship, we are still confronted with variety, because the Liturgy has taken and still takes many different forms. The point is too obvious to need illustration, although a glance at some orders of worship, prayer and service books or a visit to a number of churches even of the same denomination will quickly confirm it. The content of worship, the words that are said and sung and the sequence of events varies considerably. In some instances major items like preaching or the sharing of bread and wine are entirely omitted or relegated to an apparently minor place of importance.

Out of these many alternatives can we give any clear instructions about the one order which should be regarded as the norm? It should probably look something like this:

Greeting
A reading from the Old Testament
Psalm

A reading from a book in the New Testament other
    than the Gospels
Psalm
A reading from the Gospels
Sermon
Prayers
Offering (of gifts, including bread and wine)
Thanksgiving (variously referred to as: Eucharistic
    Prayer, Canon, Prayer of Consecration)
Breaking of bread (Fraction)
Sharing of bread and wine (Communion)
Dismissal

It is possible to argue that other items should be included such as a
confession of the church's faith (later known as a Creed) after the
sermon; and the kiss of peace or Pax before the offering. The order
given above certainly represents the barest possible outline of the
Liturgy, sometimes referred to as the service of Word and Sacrament, with its readings from the Bible followed by exposition and
preaching in the first part, and the Lord's Supper in the second. But
bare bones have their advantages! If a 'norm' for worship implies a
pattern which should be followed and certain ingredients which
should always be there, it does not impose a rigid uniformity. This
skeleton structure can be filled out in different ways. For example, by
adding mainly hymns the bare bones can be turned into a 'hymn-
sandwich' if that is what is wanted, and the result could be something
like this (the skeleton is indicated by *italics*):

Call to Worship   (*Greeting*)
Prayer of Invocation
Hymn
Old Testament Lesson
Hymn or metrical *Psalm*
New Testament Lesson
Sermon
Hymn
Prayers of Intercession (linked with the announcements)
Collection and *Offering*
Hymn
Prayer of *Thanksgiving*
Breaking
Distribution and *Sharing*

Hymn
Benediction (*Dismissal*)

The order here is certainly different from the old stereotypes of Free Church worship. The sermon has lost its place at the end as the point to which the whole service tends to move, though that does not mean that it has lost its importance. Again the communion service, instead of being treated as a separate entity or optional extra after the main service, has become part of the whole. But apart from that, loyalty to the norm need not rob Free Church worship of its distinctive character, its hymn singing and free prayer and its particular brand of preaching, where these are still treasured as meaningful and important.

On the other hand, the same skeleton may be filled out to look very different indeed. The following is a sketchy outline of the Order of Mass found in the little mass books used widely in Roman Catholic churches and distributed for use by members of the congregation (the skeleton is again indicated by *italics*).

ENTRANCE RITE
>   *Greeting*
>   Prayers—Penitence
>   　　　　　Absolution
>   　　　　　Preparation

LITURGY OF THE WORD
>   *O.T. Lesson*
>   *Psalm*
>   *Epistle*
>   Alleluia and response
>   *Gospel*
>   "The HOMILY follows for which the people sit down" (*Sermon*)
>   The Creed
>   *Prayers* of Intercession

LITURGY OF THE EUCHARIST
>   The *Offertory*
>   Preface to Eucharistic Prayer
>   Eucharistic Prayer (*Thanksgiving*)

COMMUNION RITE
>   during the first part:
>   "Agnus Dei is sung or said, and may be repeated until the *breaking of the bread* is completed"

6

COMMUNION OF THE FAITHFUL   (*Sharing*)
    Prayer after Communion
    Blessing and *Dismissal*

This outline only hints at the more elaborate nature of the service in this particular case, but it does indicate that the basic norm which is to be observed allows for a wide measure of variety, and this variety can be pursued and enjoyed all the more freely precisely because of the underlying unity. Other examples, for instance the recent Methodist order, significantly called *The* Sunday Service, could be quoted. It reveals the same essential structure in yet another form, as do the alternative orders for Holy Communion known as Second Series and Third Series (published by the Church of England in 1967 and 1971), and the more avant garde Freedom Meal of the Free Church of Berkeley, California. For a final example, take the Liturgy of St Mark's in the Bowery, New York, which stands up to repetition more than most experimental forms. (The full details can be found in *But that I can't believe* by J. A. T. Robinson, published by Fontana, pp. 112–116.) The outline is much the same as before but the act of thanksgiving is worth quoting in full. It includes most of the recurring features of this important and often complicated prayer found in liturgies old and new. We shall indicate in brackets what these features are.

(a. Introductory dialogue leading to the Preface or first part of the thanksgiving. The people are first invited to thank God for all that he has done in the past, and then proceed to do so.)
PRESIDENT: Lift up your hearts
ASSEMBLY: We lift them to the Lord.
PRESIDENT: Let us give thanks for God's glory
ASSEMBLY: We give thanks, we rejoice in the glory of all creation.
PRESIDENT: All glory be to you, O Father, who sent your only Son into the world to be a man, born of a woman's womb, to die for us on a cross that was made by us.
ASSEMBLY: He came for us. Help us to accept his coming.
PRESIDENT: He walked among us, a man, on our earth, in our world of conflict, and commanded us to remember his death, his death which gives us life; and to wait for him until he comes again in glory.
ASSEMBLY: We remember his death; we live by his presence; we wait for his coming.

(b. The Narrative of the Institution, based on I Corinthians 11.23–26
and quoted as the church's authority for observing the Lord's
Supper.)

PRESIDENT: On the night he was betrayed, the Lord Jesus took
bread, he gave thanks; he broke it, and gave it to his disciples,
saying, "Take, eat, this is my body. Do this in remembrance of me."
He also took the cup; he gave thanks; and gave it to them, saying,
"Drink of it, all of you; this is my blood of the covenant, which is
poured out for many for the forgiveness of sins."

ASSEMBLY: Come, Lord Jesus, come.

(c. The Anamnesis, which means a memorial or act of remembrance.
By offering bread and wine the church stirs up memories of past
events which become active again in the present.)

PRESIDENT: Therefore, remembering his death, believing in his
rising from the grave, longing to recognise his presence; now in this
place, we obey his command; we offer bread and wine, we offer
ourselves, to be used.

ASSEMBLY: Everything is yours, O Lord; we return the gift
which first you gave us.

(d. The Epiklesis, which means an invocation. God is asked to send
the Holy Spirit upon the bread and wine and the reason for the
request is stated.)

PRESIDENT: Accept it, Father. Send down the spirit of life and
power, glory and love, upon these people, upon this bread and wine,
that to us they may be his body and his blood.

ASSEMBLY: Come, risen Lord, live in us that we may live in you.

(e. The last part is reminiscent of a hymn called the Sanctus though
it usually comes earlier before the Narrative of the Institution.)

PRESIDENT: Now with all men who ever were, are, and will be,
with all creation in all time, with joy we sing:

PRESIDENT AND ASSEMBLY: Holy, Holy, Holy, Lord God
Almighty, all space and all time show forth your glory now and
always. Amen.

So much for the basic pattern. But why should we be reasonably
content if the Liturgy conforms to it and regard it as being inadequate
if it does not? What are our grounds for recommending this particular scheme of Word and Sacrament, readings, preaching, and
the four actions of offering, thanksgiving, breaking and sharing, out
of all the possibilities that could be mentioned?

No doubt a good deal of evidence, biblical and theological, could be assembled, but that is a little like being wise after the event. The answer is rather more untidy. The fact is that for a number of reasons a certain way of doing things developed in practice without anyone first working it out very carefully in theory on the basis of a correct theology or a biblical pattern.

What emerged has been tested by the lengthy experience of the church, which does not mean that all Christians have always done it this way. They have not. For considerable periods the normative pattern has been lost sight of and on occasions it has been deliberately discarded, but in the long run the church's accumulated wisdom has seen fit to uphold or return to it for her distinctive and central act of worship.

We are witnessing such a return at the present time, though alongside of it is a second movement which often appears to be diametrically opposed to the first. The first shows renewed admiration for a long tradition in the church. The second is disenchanted with what it regards as traditional ways of worship and looks for something fresh. It is often mistaken in calling 'traditional' what may be dated but belongs only to a comparatively recent past, but it would be a pity if either movement were to flourish at the expense of the other. We shall only find the right kind of freedom to experiment in a certain bondage to the basic pattern.

This does not mean that all that is old is good, any more than all that is new. Nor does it mean that it must be done just because it has always been done. Nor do we suggest that the pattern is beyond criticism. What we do in the church is always open to questioning by men and women who come to it with new eyes and fresh insights. It can always be challenged by the creative and disturbing pressures which come to us through the world, as well as through the life and worship of the Christian community, and above all through paying continuous and careful attention to the Scriptures.

Even the basic pattern must be open to the possibility of reformation, but that does not allow us to set aside lightly something which has persisted for so long and which hindsight reveals to be closely in touch with the bedrock of the whole Christian enterprise.

The story of how the norm developed in practice probably begins with the fellowship of the very first Christians referred to in such passages as Acts 2.42–7. It was only natural that they should meet and it was part of the very genius of what they had so recently discovered that they should share what they had, including their meals.

These meals together would be suitable occasions for helping the less well off and making sure, for example, that everyone had enough to eat (see Acts 6.1–6).

Such meals, so close in time to the events which had centred on Jesus, the only reason for meeting at all, would be rich in associations. They could hardly fail to bring to mind the meals that some of them ate with him after the Resurrection, and all the other ordinary meals that they had eaten together during his ministry. Some were more memorable than others—two above all. One was the occasion when five thousand people were miraculously fed on the most inadequate provisions, turning a fast into a feast which seemed about as good as the banquet that was promised in the Kingdom of God.

The other was the supper in the upper room in Jerusalem just before Jesus died, when he had given to some of the conventional customs which surrounded Jewish eating habits a new and quite special significance. The main meal, though, if it was Passover, not the whole proceedings, would begin as usual with grace. The host took break and broke it as he said: "Blessed be Thou, O Lord our God, Eternal King, Who bringest forth bread from the earth." He would then eat a fragment himself and give a piece to all who were present. But as Jesus did what anyone else would have done, he added a comment: "This is my body, which is for you; do this as a memorial of me." After the meal, with its several courses, hands were washed (or perhaps on that one occasion feet were washed, and by the host who was like a servant) and then followed a second and much longer grace which thanked God for all his gifts, but above all for his goodness to the Jews in bringing them out of Egypt at the Exodus and making a covenant with them. On special occasions this grace was said over the 'cup of blessing' which was then sipped by the host and passed round. As Jesus followed the conventional procedure he added a second comment: "This cup is the new covenant sealed by my blood. Whenever you drink it, do this as a memorial of me."

Now these early Christians found themselves doing just that. Because Christ had risen and eaten with them since his death, they shared their meals, no doubt observing the usual customs, but 'with unaffected joy' believing that he was with them as he had been before, and looking forward, as he had done, to the great banquet in the final Kingdom of God. In their excitement they were convinced that that day was not far ahead and that they would not have to wait very long. The risen and ascended Christ would soon return.

The dominant mood would have been very gay indeed and a far cry from the atmosphere which usually descends on our communion services, where one gets the impression that to be serious you have to be solemn and that anything remotely cheerful is out of place. Theirs was not a memorial service for a dead friend. It was not even a wake to drown their sorrows. They had much to be grateful for and good reason to celebrate, which does not mean that they indulged in cheap gaiety which knows nothing of the darker side of life.

They did not forget. They knew that their new-found hope was only possible because of the body which had been given for them on the cross, and that a new covenant had come into being and a new era opened up at the expense of a life and the painful shedding of blood.

Some have thought that whereas the early stories conjure up pictures of simple fellowship meals somewhat intoxicated by the spirit of the Resurrection, Paul presents a rather different picture in I Corinthians 11.23–26 which emphasises the grimmer aspects of the affair: "For every time you eat this bread and drink this cup, you proclaim the death of the Lord, until he comes." But there is no good reason to question Paul's claim that this tradition which he handed on could be traced back to the beginning, along with the rest. It was 'received from the Lord'. If his ideas tended to dominate they were certainly not new. The Resurrection was inseparable from the cross.

The meals they shared then were full of associations and not least the memory of the Last Supper and the events which immediately followed, making all too much sense of what Jesus had said.

After a time it looks as though those customary Jewish graces to which Jesus had given new significance became separated from the meal which was eaten in between. The meal became known as the Love-feast or Agape, and what was left, the Eucharist or thanksgiving. What other name could be given to a grace at meal times?

Some think that the separation was unfortunate or that it is a pity that at least on more informal occasions we do not follow this primitive practice of celebrating the Lord's Supper within the context of a meal 'in private houses'. But we shall return to that.

Good or bad, the separation of the Agape from the Eucharist probably explains why we find ourselves with four items in our basic Liturgy when we might have expected—and in some churches still find—seven.

11

The Gospels report that Jesus did seven things on that night before he was betrayed:

1 He took bread
2 He gave thanks
3 He broke it
4 He gave it to them
5 He took a cup
6 He gave thanks
7 He gave it to them

But remember that between actions 4 and 5, the first grace and the second, came all the courses of a meal and all the time it took. Remove the meal and the two thanksgivings now become one, and the seven actions are understandably reduced to four:

1 He took bread and a cup
2 He gave thanks
3 He broke the bread
4 He gave the bread and the cup to the disciples

These are represented in the basic norm of the Liturgy by

Offering
Thanksgiving (Eucharistic Prayer, Canon, Prayer of Consecration)
Breaking of bread (Fraction)
Sharing of bread and wine (Communion)

For the most part they are, in origin, what they say they are. The thanksgiving is an expression of gratitude for all that God has done for us in making the world and caring for his people. If the Jewish grace reached its climax in grateful recollection of the Exodus, the Christian grace reaches its climax in gratefully recalling the birth, life, death and Resurrection of Jesus. After that the loaf had to be broken in order, finally, to be shared.

The word 'offering' is the only stranger. Surely it ought to be 'taking', but very soon the straightforward business of taking a loaf from the food provided for the meal in order to give thanks, break and share it, became associated with other ideas. The food that was brought, which included bread and wine, came to be seen as an offering made by the Christian worshippers to God, an offering which could represent the whole of life, including themselves.

12

What happened to the taking of bread and wine and turned it into the offering would happen to all four actions. These simple procedures began to carry all sorts of ideas, not so much by importing new ones as by unpacking and drawing out the implications of what was already there. The broken bread, for example, came to be a dramatic reminder of the way the Lord's body was in fact broken, whereas originally he only said of the bread "This is my body" and broke it in order to share it. The shared loaf and the common cup became acted parables of the unity of Christian believers made one by their common sharing in the life of Christ (I Cor. 10.16 f.). It was especially important to explain this to Gentile Christians. Unaware of Jewish customs, they may never have seen what Jews took for granted: that to share bread was to make ties between you. The prayer of thanksgiving, which was often a free prayer, became greatly elaborated. Paul's words of Institution (I Cor. 11) were included and have been ever since. Additional prayers reflected more than one understanding of what was being done.

But such elaboration and the association of many ideas with these simple actions only illustrates the marvellous ability of the basic norm to provide us with an act of worship in which all can share together, with a welcome opportunity for variety, in this case, of interpretation.

However, we are beginning to look at the scenery when our primary purpose is to offer a few clear instructions to guide the traveller. We are looking at how the basic norm developed in practice. We have seen how the early Christians arrived at the characteristic pattern of offering, thanksgiving, breaking and sharing. This is no more than a crude and simplified version of a very complicated story, and it also leaves half the story untold.

The first Christians as we know were all Jews. They already had certain forms of worship. They continued, for example, to go to the Temple, though Temple worship was not what it once was. Officially it may still have held the place of honour, but it was of less importance in practice. The synagogue was a more regular and significant feature of the lives of most Jews.

When a Jew went to the synagogue he would find a familiar and regular order of service. It had four main ingredients. First there was the public reading of the Scriptures, which of course for them meant the Old Testament. Second, there were Psalms set to music. Third, there was a sermon or teaching based on the Scriptures and expounding their meaning, and fourth there were prayers, some of them written down and others more freely composed .

13

It was this synagogue service which provided the framework for the other part of the basic norm of the Liturgy: the Scripture readings interspersed with Psalms, the sermon and the prayers. The Scriptures would now include the uncollected new writings of the apostles, their letters to the young churches, the sayings of Jesus and the stories about him; and the sermon would have rather more to say than the president of the synagogue had ever imagined!

We could be forgiven for thinking that these two parts of Christian worship, one associated with a meal and the other with the synagogue, came together from the start. "They met constantly to hear the apostles teach, and to share the common life, to break bread, and to pray." (Acts 2.42). They may have been practised together at times. They were almost certainly practised separately at times. But separately or together they were both part of the life of the young church from its earliest days. They have drifted apart more than once in the last 1,900 years, giving rise to criticisms of Eucharists and Masses at which the Word has not been adequately read and preached, and of preaching services which have become impoverished because the Sacrament has been ignored or given worse than second place.

But in those early centuries they received more equal respect and normally went together, and it is the judgment of Christian experience that this unity of Word and Sacrament is a seamless robe which should not lightly be torn in two.

So far we have looked only at the way in which the bare bones of the Liturgy took shape and have hinted that as time went on they became greatly elaborated by other ideas, words and actions. How well did the basic pattern survive? What happened after those early years?

We cannot embark on even a potted history of Christian worship, but we ought to enter a plea for a sense of perspective. So often we work with a peculiarly shortened view of the story of the church, as if it consisted of the New Testament period and what we can remember of the more recent past, particularly within our own traditions. If we know that there is a great deal more to it than that, we hide that awareness fairly successfully.

Over the past 2,000 years the skeletal pattern can be discerned more often than not in the Eastern churches as well as in the West. That does not mean that worship has always been satisfactory. At times the Liturgy has been both misunderstood and badly misused. The Middle Ages for example are not the most glorious chapters of its history and at the end of them men like Luther and Calvin were

14

well aware of the need for reform. Amongst other things they restored the Bible and preaching to a place of honour. They also insisted, though without a great deal of success, that it was essential for the people to share the bread and the wine with the priest.

It is only in some traditions and in comparatively recent times that the pattern has virtually disappeared. The Book of Common Prayer of 1662, though all too reminiscent for some of the ways of Rome, is badly at fault as far as the four actions are concerned. Sharing is placed in the middle of the thanksgiving, and offering and breaking are difficult to find. On the continent Zwingli openly rejected the unity of Word and Sacrament, relegating the latter to an occasional observance and adopting a quite different order of service for normal Sunday use. The Puritans inherited the basic pattern from Calvin and even when the Sacrament was omitted they followed the pattern as far as they could, leaving out only those items which actually involved the bread and the wine. We sometimes refer to what was left as 'ante-communion'. It was probably in the heat of their quarrel with the establishment, leading up to the Act of Uniformity in 1662, that they eventually abandoned it and turned their sympathies toward those movements which had long since separated from the Church of England and were even more sceptical of its traditions. In their worship the skeletal pattern we have talked about was hard to see, and that is frequently still the case among their descendants in the so-called Free Churches of England. But even here, under the influence of the Liturgical Movement (see page 64 f.), greatly helped by better tools for historical research, efforts to recover it have long been under way and are steadily gaining ground.

We must not draw false conclusions or overstate the case, but the norm has proved to be more persistent than we might imagine when we see things from the perspective of our own rather narrow horizons.

It will be clear that its justification does not depend in any simple way on the Bible. Some have thought that it should. The Puritans are a notable example. They disliked the Book of Common Prayer because its reforms did not go far enough. Scripture was to be the criterion for everything and they agreed with Calvin that worship should only contain what Scripture specifically ordained. One result was that the four actions of offering, thanksgiving, breaking and sharing were replaced by the seven we referred to previously, and the Lord's Supper became a repetition of the Last Supper. This misunderstanding still survives and it is a far cry from what the Resurrection meals were all about.

But if some have thought that the details of worship should have direct scriptural authority, they also found that, as with so many other aspects of Christian faith and practice, this is a very difficult ideal to achieve and one which is riddled with problems. In the main the church did not take her instructions from the New Testament in this way, and could not have done so even if she had tried. Her worship was rapidly developing and took on its essential characteristics before the New Testament existed in the complete and authoritative form in which we have it today. Indeed to some extent the reverse was the case. The worship of the early church had some responsibility for the form and contents of the New Testament which eventually emerged.

If the basic pattern of worship we have described is to be taken seriously it is out of respect for the tradition of the church, by which we mean its developing practice and accumulated wisdom, tested by experience and guided by the Spirit of God at work in and through her life.

However, it is one thing to say that we do not go to the Bible for direct and detailed instructions, but quite another to suggest that the distinctive act of Christian worship should be unbiblical and contrary to its general teaching. If we do not agree with the Puritans and Calvin that worship can only contain what Scripture specifically ordains, we should want to go further than saying that we can allow anything that it does not specifically exclude. It must exert a more positive influence than that, and worship, like the church, must always live with the Bible and keep itself open to correction and reformation according to the Word of God.

More than once exciting things have happened when that essential rule has been observed. This safeguard must be written into the church's regular and on-going life. It is here we find an additional reason for commending the basic pattern of the Liturgy. It is justified mainly out of respect for the accumulated wisdom and experience of the Christian community, but no one can deny that it gives a firm and important place to the reading of the Bible. The Liturgy itself is in constant touch with the very ground of the church's existence, a point we shall find of some significance as we go on to offer further basic directions.

Telling the Story

So far we have suggested that amongst the many services we could think of, there is one which has a special place as the distinctive act of Christian worship. We have called it the Liturgy. It has taken many different forms but the tradition of the church calls our attention to an underlying skeletal pattern which should be characteristic of them all.

But even when this basic norm is accepted and the Christian community gathers to do the Liturgy, there are many different ways not only of doing it but of understanding what exactly is being done.

There is little point in looking at them in order to decide which one is right out of all the rest. Like a major work of art, the Liturgy is capable of bearing more than one explanation which we can acknowledge as valuable and true. We may often wish to compare and criticise but we do not wish to exclude.

If, for the guidance of the traveller, we single out one understanding of what is being done from among so many, we shall try to fasten on to what is distinctive about the Liturgy in a way which is acceptable to most Christians and which does not rule out a perfectly proper variety of opinion.

A glance at the 'bare bones' referred to in the previous section reveals that its most prominent features are not the hymns, prayers, litanies and creeds we so often associate with services, but the Word, which includes the lessons, psalms and sermon, and the Sacrament with its four familiar actions. In different ways they all attract our attention to what we shall refer to as the Story.

It is known well enough to most of us. It concerns a young Palestinian Jew who lived out most of his days in obscurity but who, during his last years, came into the public eye. He delighted many by his activities as he travelled about teaching, healing and making friends. He also made enemies and met with increasing hostility. Eventually he was brought to the notice of the Roman authorities. On somewhat dubious evidence he was found guilty of a capital offence. He died at the hands of the Roman executioner at about thirty-three years of age. A few days later his close associates and admirers were convinced that he was alive. From these central events the Story widens out in many directions. Behind it, as it were, is its setting in the history of the Jewish people. Moving forward it has its immediate and long term consequences in the story of the Christian church and of the world at large, but the main pre-occupation of the bare bones of the Liturgy is with those central events concerning Jesus of Nazareth.

The Scripture readings are a clear example. The Bible cannot be simply equated with the Story, not even the four Gospels which

17

concentrate most obviously on the life of Jesus. The Bible includes some of the earliest attempts to put the significance of the Story into words and to work out its implications in practical terms. Some of its interpretations have been read back into the Story itself and have affected the way it is told. The result is usually enriching, not misleading. The Bible is not the Story, but it contains the earliest, and in the church's opinion the most reliable reactions to what took place and can be regarded as the safest strong box in which the Story is kept secure.

The Liturgy requires us to read three passages, one from the Old Testament and two from the New. One of these is from the Gospels, and little ceremonies, such as standing while it was read, soon grew up at this point as if to emphasise its peculiar importance.

All too often we make do with one, or at the most two, readings instead of three. We are content with a few verses instead of an extract of reasonable length, and perhaps worst of all, we tend to restrict our reading to a small number of well-known paragraphs or repeatedly select those parts we like the best. It is very easy to obtain and follow a carefully worked out scheme for reading the Bible. It is called a lectionary, and it makes sure that over one or two years, Sunday by Sunday, all the main parts are covered without ignoring the fact that some are not worth reading at all and some are more important than others.

After the readings comes the sermon. We cannot embark on a full discussion of preaching here. We must be content to state a point of view which is closely related to our understanding of the Liturgy. There is room for others and we shall return to at least one of them later.

The word 'sermon' has tended to cover a multitude of sins. It can refer to almost any address given from a pulpit. The preacher may venture a Christian opinion on matters of the day. Too frequently he upbraids the congregation for their shortcomings as individuals and as members of the church, and reminds them of their duty. At best this shows a poor understanding of human nature. Those who have tried and failed usually need fresh resources not repeated instructions to go and try again.

The sermon should be less concerned with what we ought to do than with what has already been done. Preaching is proclamation. It announces the good news about what has happened, and what has happened is that Jesus has been born, has lived among men, was crucified and on the third day was raised from the dead. The incompleteness and promise of the Old Testament point towards these

18

events and the Gospels and Epistles arise out of them. The scriptural readings and sermon can be of a piece as the preacher moves the people on from the Old Testament or helps them to penetrate the doctrinal and ethical teaching of the New Testament to focus their attention on those events which hold them together. The preacher's task is to help men to see Jesus. He is primarily a storyteller.

The same Story confronts us when we turn to the four actions of the Sacrament. We have already seen that the major concern of the thanksgiving is to rehearse all that God has done for us from the time "when all things began". In particular, in what is known as the anamnesis or memorial, it gratefully commemorates the Passion and Resurrection of Jesus. It also includes the words of Paul referring to the night when he was betrayed. It remembers the Story and gives thanks. Even if nothing were to be said, what is done would be a sharp enough reminder of the same events. "Do this in remembrance of me." From the very first, as we have seen, this Christian meal, enriched by its pointed references to the Last Supper, was inextricably associated with all that happened. For many Christians, especially in the Eastern churches, those associations have extended to the Incarnation, and for all Christians they have certainly included the crucifixion which followed that unforgettable occasion in the upper room, and the Resurrection appearances when they found Jesus breaking bread with them again.

If we reduce the Liturgy, as we have done, to its barest outline, and then ask what is its central concern, a possible answer is that in readings from the Bible, the proclamation of good news, thankful recollection and actions, it is concerned to tell the Story.

The Liturgy has tried to do that in other ways as well. For example, in the East where it was not always possible to hear the Story and take a full share in worship, the congregation was taught to read the Story into all that was going on. When the bread and wine were being prepared out of sight before the service began, the people were to think of the birth of Jesus and the hidden years of his childhood and youth. When the Gospel was carried in to be read, at what was known as the Little Entrance (notice the ceremony surrounding this most important reading) they were to see Jesus emerging from obscurity into his public ministry. At the Great Entrance, when the bread and wine were taken in procession through the congregation (the offering) Christ is on his way to suffering and death. As the gifts are laid on the table he is buried in his tomb. At the consecration of the bread and wine (part of the thanksgiving) the thoughts of the people turn to the Resurrection and when the chalice is brought to them for communion, the risen Christ appears to his disciples. The blessing at the end of the service is the blessing of the ascended Lord. Here in action, but traditionally in the outline of the Liturgy, week by week the Story is told.

If this is our understanding of what is being done then it could be objected that we have given a very poor account of worship indeed. Let us take a well known particular example which has universal appeal as a paradigm of what worship is all about. It is the prophet's experience in the Temple as reported in Isaiah 6:

> In the year that King Uzziah died I saw the Lord sitting upon a throne, high and lifted up; and his train filled the temple. Above him stood the seraphim; each had six wings: with two he covered his face, and with two he covered his feet, and with two he flew. One called to another and said:
> "Holy, holy, holy is the Lord of hosts; the whole earth is full of his glory."
> And the foundations of the thresholds shook at the voice of him who called, and the house was filled with smoke. And I said, "Woe is me! For I am lost; for I am a man of unclean lips, and I dwell in the midst of a people of unclean lips; for my eyes have seen the King, the Lord of hosts!"
> Then flew one of the seraphim to me, having in his hand a burning coal which he had taken with tongs from the altar. And he touched my mouth, and said: "Behold, this has touched your lips; your guilt is taken away, and your sin is forgiven." And I heard the voice of the Lord saying, "Whom shall I send, and who will go for us?" Then I said, "Here I am! Send me." (R.S.V.)

After which the prophet is sent on his somewhat daunting mission.

There are at least three aspects of that experience which we have not referred to. First, in worship the prophet encountered a God who was felt to be very much alive and whose presence was overwhelming. Second, he was recreated or renewed. Made all too aware of his uncleanness, he was conscious that he had been forgiven. This was not a selfish experience. It did not merely make him feel better and glad that he'd been to church. He was renewed for service and he left the Temple not only with a blessing but also with a commission. He was sent away on God's business. It might help us to go and do likewise if a dismissal replaced the benediction at the end of the Liturgy. Third, this experience of worship was a natural opportunity for the prophet to make an offering, not of an animal in the tradition of temple worship, but of himself. "Here I am! Send me."

Encounter with God, the renewal of our lives for mission, and the offering of ourselves. We need only look at other parts of the Bible, at prayer books, orders of service, hymns and some of the words associated with worship to find abundant evidence that those experiences have been widely shared by Christian people. Are not these much more satisfactory understandings of what we are doing, and is not the idea of 'Telling the Story' a rather poor alternative?

Two things need to be said. First, from the start we set our faces against excluding other explanations. We were more concerned to indicate as clearly as we could what is distinctive about the Liturgy rather than to say everything there is to say about worship, and the view that we have taken is in no sense incompatible with an understanding of worship as encounter with God, or renewal or offering.

As a matter of fact the idea of offering is already there within the basic pattern, though as we have seen it was an early elaboration of the necessary business of taking the bread and wine in order to share them. Even without the offering as such, the very fact of telling the Story implies a commitment to it and its implications, and the giving of ourselves to the reality of which it speaks.

We encounter God in many ways, most of them outside of organised services altogether, and it is perfectly possible to believe, as many Christians do, that the encounter which provides the pattern for all the rest is experienced through the Word and Sacrament which make up our basic norm. As for the renewal of our lives, and the remaking of the Christian community to share in God's work in the world, one of the fundamental attractions of the Story is the belief that in it lies the hope of our salvation and the making of all things new.

Telling the Story can be an encounter with the God who is like Jesus. It can offer us new resources and be an opportunity for commitment. But second, if these ideas are compatible with the Liturgy, and have indeed become integral parts of Christian worship, I venture the opinion that no one of them should be exalted as the basic understanding of what we are doing. For example, the Liturgy should not become, by definition, the worship of God. These ideas are accepted and welcomed by many of us, but they are not absolute requirements for sharing in the Liturgy. A certain amount of choice is open to us. We can be committed to the business of telling the Story without being necessarily committed to these other additional explanations. I say this with a fair number of people in mind who have a good deal of difficulty, intellectual and experiential, in viewing worship for example as an encounter with God or regarding it as a recreative experience. Their frame of mind, conditioned by a long history of ideas in the West, finds it well-nigh impossible to conceive of God's existence. The problems are by now familiar enough. If God is not a concept which we have outgrown, and that is still a possibility, then he has to be thought of in a different way and a way which few may have found with any degree of confidence.

Disenchantment with worship as a recreating experience has led many to give it up or search for viable alternatives. Life without it appears to carry on as before. Worship has few positive results and one often feels bored rather than better after attending. Recreation is looked for elsewhere.

This disappointment is aggravated by our impatience with anything that is not immediately seen to work, and by the subjective tendencies of so much Christian worship for so long. It has encouraged us to be preoccupied with ourselves and how we feel. We should not despise our feelings but we should not rely on them too much. The weakness of some contemporary experiments is that we try to overcome our disappointment with worship by making the same mistakes and simply finding a new formula which promises instant renewal and makes us feel good.

Difficulties of this kind may or may not be easily sustained, but they are felt, and one has sympathy with those who feel them. If the Liturgy must be understood in terms of worshipping God, or is to be judged by its success as a recreative experience, then, on their present understanding of these things, it is not for them. That would be a pity if despite such hesitations, they were still attracted by and prepared to give their allegiance to Jesus and his Story.

It is this which appears to be distinctively Christian. The earliest Christian confession may have operated within a framework of certain metaphysical ideas, but it did not require them. It declared only that 'Jesus is Lord'.

The Christian faith has given rise to a host of doctrinal and theological systems, but they are not at its heart in the same way as the Story of Jesus. "When all is said and done, the Christian community consists of those people who keep on telling this story to each other, and some of those people climb up on soap boxes of some kind to tell the story to others." (Peter Berger: *Christian Century*. 27th Feb. 1971.) They tell it to each other in the Liturgy, the most distinctive of all their activities. If we cannot accept a great deal but want to accept this, then we ought not to be excluded from being the Jesus people, if not for the time being the people of God.

The Liturgy then is not necessarily understood as the worship of God. It is nevertheless an act of worship or 'worth-ship'. Here we affirm the worth of the Story by telling it. Here we acknowledge that its hero is our Lord and that as far as we are concerned nothing surpasses it in the significance which it holds for our lives. The Liturgy may or may not be understood as an encounter with God but it remains an encounter not merely with the projection of our own ideas but with events that are independent and not part of us, adding to the sum total of our experience, offering us gifts and making demands. In committing ourselves to the Liturgy we offer or give ourselves to live by the Story that is told, and whilst we may not always feel any immediate benefit and do not judge the Liturgy on that score, we believe that in telling the Story we have to do with the creative and renewing springs of life and the gracious resources we need so much.

The Story itself is not a realist's reproduction of the facts. It is an interpretative account of events and is often impressionist in character. Even the telling of it can be an interpretation, and once heard it can be added to, enriched and understood in various ways. But in the midst of all this variety, the Story which is told by means of the bare bones of the Liturgy finds us all on common ground. It is the point at which we can meet beyond or before our various interpretations of worship, or of Jesus and the outlook he inspires, begin to divide us up. Even when they do, it remains the point at which we can stay together, doing the same Liturgy, telling the same Story, committed to the same Lord, whilst interpreting all these things in many different ways.

This Christian community is rather like the assorted crowd which gathers round a notable painting in a gallery. They have arrived in front of it for various reasons. They understand the whole business of going to art galleries in various ways. For some it is a natural thing to do, for others it is strange; some enjoy going, for others it has become a habit. One or two have simply come in out of the rain.

They see different things in the picture, but they are all attracted by it. They like it, in fact they are greatly impressed. It is not merely decorative. Everyone senses that it has extraordinary significance, though each one's account of it would differ from the next.

The crowd represents a wide variety of attitudes, ways of thinking, motives and patterns of understanding, but they share, quite objectively, a picture on the wall and their confession that it has become important to them. Those who do not agree here move on.

The Christian picture has attracted a crowd week after week for generations. It is not on a wall but in a Story. The Story is told in the Liturgy with its basic pattern of Word and Sacrament, and that Liturgy is the characteristic act of the church.

The status quo

At a time when many are impatient with church services and are searching for new forms of worship, the preceding pages will probably sound very conservative and not unlike an argument for the status quo. The bare bones look like very dry bones indeed. Here is the kind of worship we must move away from rather than return to or reinforce. Let me underline one or two points already made and add one or two more.

As far as the bare bones of the Liturgy are concerned, we have argued for a very old and in many ways a very traditional basic structure, but other considerations qualify its rather staid image. These bare bones can put on flesh in many different ways. The old normative outline can take a contemporary form, and this does not mean merely adding other things. We have been concerned to perpetuate what has traditionally been done, but we are not concerned to perpetuate the traditional ways of doing it, or rather the ways in which it has been done in comparatively recent years. To insist on preaching, for example, is not necessarily to insist on a twenty minute monologue. We can do different things, but we can also do the same things differently!

It might be argued that however it is done, this Liturgy would still be far removed from the present day. It would incur the charge of irrelevance. We must take up later the question of relating worship to contemporary life, but it can be said straight away that no one would suppose for a moment that it is enough to tell the Story, however much telling it might imply about our priorities and commitments. It is meaningless to say of anything that it is important unless we begin to say why. The Story is not all that has to be said.

On the other hand it is fair to suggest that what is often felt to be irrelevant at the present time is not the Story itself but so much of the baggage it has picked up en route from the first century to the twentieth and which Christians are not necessarily required to carry at all. Some of the patterns of worship we complain about for example are not traditional in the sense in which we have talked about tradition and they are not always faithful to the basic pattern we have advocated. Here, as elsewhere, the radical move is not always to start from scratch and try something completely different but to go back to the roots. A return to the Story itself might be the most creative contribution to so-called relevance.

"We shall not cease from exploration
And the end of all our exploring
Will be to arrive where we started
and know the place for the first time"
T. S. Eliot: Four Quartets

Finally however, after a proper place has been given to contemporary forms of worship, and we have recognised the need to relate the Story to our own experience in this world of today, there comes a point at which we admit to the charge that what has been written is a plea for the status quo and that the position we have outlined is to some extent unashamedly conservative.

It is a matter of understanding the nature of the Christian faith. Its roots do not lie in a set of highly polished theoretical ideas, although it has given rise to a great deal of intellectual activity. Its roots lie in things that happened, which like most things that happen were not neatly ordered or theoretically reasonable, but untidy and arbitrary. It is difficult to see why it should have happened this way out of a myriad possibilities, which is not to say that those who were involved had no plans and purposes.

This sense of arbitrariness is what is sometimes referred to as 'the scandal of particularity'. A small example of it might be the insistence that bread and wine must be used in the Liturgy rather than some sensible alternatives with a local and contemporary flavour, like tea and biscuits. It may be true that God can be encountered in any and every meal and that there is urgent need to discover him within the familiar things of our everyday lives. To insist on the use of bread and wine is not to deny that. It is to make a different point. Christianity has its roots in a number of particular events which have a time and a place and involved certain people and certain things. Its nature is historical. It did not begin in someone's head or 'up there' in some ideal world, but down here on the round earth of time and space. It is tied to details. What is more, if anyone tries to replace this untidy piece of history with more manageable theories or tidy up the particularities with a few general ideas, the quality of the painting is lost. It becomes uninteresting and unimportant, and where the texture was deep there remains only a thin veneer.

As long as we wish to deal with Christianity we are stuck with certain events which form the major part of what we have called the Story. It is this Story which is rehearsed in the Liturgy, in readings, proclamation, grateful recollection and actions, and unless we change the faith we cannot change that. But, as we have suggested, it is in some such bondage, and the sense of direction which it gives, that we shall find our true freedom to appreciate and enjoy the scenery which surrounds this distinctive act of Christian worship.

II

VARIATIONS

So far we have been concerned with some permanent features of the central and distinctive act of Christian worship. By doing the Liturgy and following the basic pattern of Word and Sacrament with its scriptural readings, preaching and the four actions of offering, thanksgiving, breaking and sharing, Christians affirm that Jesus of Nazareth and the events concerning him have supreme worth or significance for their lives.

But if in this sense there is one Liturgy, there are also many. If some items on the order paper are fixed there are many more which are not. If distinctively Christian worship must always remain the same, there is about it an equally enduring and necessary variety. Even the basic pattern can be followed in a number of different ways, and around it has grown up an immense amount of material such as prayers, songs, ceremonies, creeds and dialogues as Christians have responded to the Story of Jesus. The Story itself is capable of bearing more than one interpretation which can alter the character and content of the worship it inspires.

If the fixed element has not always been respected, this variety which has surrounded it from the start has not always been approved. More than one attempt has been made to impose uniformity, though for different reasons.

The Emperor Charlemagne was attracted to it at the close of the eighth century. The English Acts of Uniformity under Elizabeth I and Charles II imposed a common prayer book, but they owed more to the political and religious struggles of the time than to considerations which had a great deal to do with worship as such. Again, the control of the Liturgy tightened in the Roman Church with the establishment of the Congregation of Sacred Rites in 1588 following the Council of Trent and the upheavals of the Reformation. But on the whole these attempts were never entirely successful, nor were they themselves prepared to exclude all variations. Absolute uniformity has proved impossible to achieve, and any fears that a greater degree of church unity might mean all of us having to worship in the same way are ill-founded in the light of Christian history. Even if it were practical we should not want it, and for much the same reasons as we should not want all racial and and social groups to have the same temperament and culture, or all human beings to have identical personalities or all Christians to understand their faith in exactly the same way. Granted that there are certain things we have in common, like the basic structure of the Liturgy, variety is as inevitable and welcome a feature of worship as it is of life.

To this variety we now turn. It exists for a number of reasons and we can only look at a few. They are all interrelated but it will help our discussion to distinguish between three of them under the following headings:

1 Historical circumstances
2 Theological differences
3 Differences of temperament

Three more historical episodes will serve to illustrate each of them in turn. Having looked at the origins of Christian worship in the shared meals of the early Christians and the synagogues of the Jews, we shall go on to describe very briefly first the differences between the pre-Nicene Liturgy and what came later, second the growing division between East and West as it is reflected in their worship, and third the eventual synthesis of what are known as the Gallican and the Roman rites.

Historical circumstances

Although the Council of Nicaea, held in A.D. 325, was important enough to give its name to the end of an era, so that we often refer to the pre or ante-Nicene church, it was not, for us, the event which mattered most. The peace which the Emperor Constantine brought to the church round about the same time had more far reaching effects on the Liturgy.

The pre-Nicene church was not always persecuted. The situation could change from one ruler to the next. Legally it was a proscribed religion with no right to exist. In practice it often enjoyed a considerable degree of toleration and was able to grow in number and in influence. But the church was always vulnerable. It was an obvious scapegoat. The troubles of the empire tended to be blamed on the Christians who had forsaken the old gods under whom Rome had prospered. The stronger the church became, and the more highly organised, the more it looked like a state within a state over which the secular power had insufficient control. It was feared as subversive and disliked by the general populace.

Feelings such as these led to bitter persecutions in the middle of the third century under Decius and Gallus and then by Decius's henchman, Valerian. His son Gallienus inaugurated an uneasy peace. The last fearful outbreak came at the beginning of the fourth century under Diocletian. Toleration came in 311 and the Edict of Milan (313) gave Christianity the same legal rights as any other religion. When Constantine finally became ruler of the East as well as the West in 323 the church found itself everywhere at peace. To what extent he himself was a Christian is not clear. His father, a governor in Gaul, had been more kindly disposed than some to the Christians during the persecutions, and Constantine himself believed that the Christian God had given him victory in battle.

Whatever the personal beliefs of the Emperor there was no mistaking the change of fortune for the church. Almost overnight the hostility of the state had turned to something more like hospitality, and the dispossessed began to look like the establishment.

Whenever persecution ceased Christian worship took on a more public character in at least two ways. First it was attended by larger numbers of people. In so far as the difference between private and public is a matter of size, once the church embraced virtually the whole population congregations were certainly too large to be thought of as private parties. Second, worship became public because it was free to come into the open. Members of the congregation were no longer wanted men who must do the Liturgy in fear of their lives. There was no need to hide for reasons of security.

Worship still remained secret in another sense. Only the fully initiated or baptised were admitted to the Eucharist. Even the catechumens who were preparing for baptism and were virtually part of the Christian community were dismissed from the Liturgy after the lessons and sermon before the prayers and the actions of the Eucharist. It was still not 'Public Worship' for all those who could possibly be persuaded to attend, though again as time went on and most people were baptised as a matter of course, there were few who qualified for exclusion. What began as a closed shop ended up as an open house. But if worship temporarily remained 'secret' and only for the initiated, it no longer needed to be secretive. It could come out of hiding into public view and the light of day.

As a result, the place of worship shifted from the private house to a public building called a church. It was now safe to do so and larger numbers made more ample accommodation a practical necessity. You could no longer squeeze the congregation into the lounge.

In the early centuries church buildings became something of a barometer, though a rather perverse one. They went up when the temperature cooled and a measure of peace and toleration made Christians feel reasonably secure. As soon as things got hot the churches were a sitting target for destruction, and down they came. In the age of Constantine they certainly went up and he himself made many generous gifts including magnificent churches in Rome, Bethlehem and Jerusalem.

What were these buildings like? Their design was undoubtedly influenced by that of the homes where Christians had previously met. These would have been the larger houses of the day and we can easily imagine how the plan of their courtyards or banqueting rooms evolved into the plan of a church. Of even more interest is the basilica, a typical public building of the day. It was basilicas which Constantine ordered to be built as churches. It was the most natural, almost conventional way of providing a place in which large numbers of people could meet.

The basilica tended to be a long and narrow building. It probably began life as an open courtyard surrounded by colonnades and a covered walkway. When it was later roofed in, the width of the building was limited to the distance the builders could span. A wooden beam could only go so far. The building could be enlarged by adding aisles or a lean-to at the side, but the main and central part could only be made bigger by being made longer.

Another feature to notice is the platform and, very often, the rounded apse at one end of the building. The basilica began life as the throne room or audience chamber of the *basileus* or monarch, and the platform was where he sat. His throne in the apse at the end of the long hall with its rows of pillars, together with the splendid clothes and rich decorations would have made an impressive sight to see. It was meant to impress.

The building was later used for other occasions and, rather like a town hall, was a convenient place to conduct various pieces of public business; but its original character and associations remained and they had their effect on Christian worship. It was true that Christians had never had purpose-built meeting places and had used what was to hand. In this sense there was no great change. The basilica was the obvious type of building to use; but it was a very different type from what they had used before, and far from worship dictating what kind

30

of building it should be, the kind of building tended to dictate what kind of worship it would house.

The sheer size of the place put certain limitations on what could be done. What was possible with a group was not necessarily possible with a crowd. The old domestic intimacy was lost. The shape of the building was also influential. Previously the table and the president of the Eucharist had been relatively near to all who were there. Now they were far more remote, at the end of a long narrow hall. The Liturgy no longer took place amongst the people but 'up the front' and they were invited only to watch from a distance. In the house the worship room had been a stage and all the congregation had a share in the liturgical play, even if some were only walking-on parts. Basilicas had never been designed for active participation, and the majority were expected to retire from the stage, now reduced to a platform at one end, and leave the acting to someone else. For perhaps the first time there was a passive audience at Christian worship. People listened but did not take part.

Added to all this were the building's associations. Just as we are still inclined to behave in a particular way when we get inside a church, so they felt there was a proper way to behave inside the basilica. It was associated with grand and ceremonious occasions, impressive displays, formality. An appropriate measure of respect was expected of those who attended. This was not without its uses. It effectively communicated to a nominally Christian populace that the Liturgy, like an interview with the monarch, was something to be taken very seriously, but it introduced a note of awe probably absent from those more informal occasions in the house.

When worship moved into public buildings it was turned from a private party into a public meeting. The occasion became much more formal. What went on seemed much more remote. It was no longer an activity in which everybody shared but one at which most were now spectators. A Liturgy emerged which differed a great deal, at least in style, from the Liturgy of the pre-Nicene church. We might experience something of the difference if we went first to a communion service celebrated round the dining table in a large suburban house, where everybody knew everybody else, and then on to a celebration of High Mass in a small provincial cathedral built in the basilican tradition and packed to the doors.

The changes we have referred to were not all apparent at once and it was no doubt centuries before people became consciously aware of them. But another way of worshipping was beginning to emerge.

Variety was growing up. The new features were hardly born out of new convictions about the nature of the Christian Liturgy. They happened almost by accident. They can be traced back in large measure to the changed historical circumstances in which Christians found themselves when toleration came to the church, spasmodically in the second and third centuries and more lastingly in the reign of Constantine.

Theological differences
We have looked at the effect of the oblong basilica on the Liturgy. A tradition of round church buildings grew up in the East. They originated as tombs (or martyria) in honour of the early Christian martyrs and were built alongside the basilicas for worship. Later, and with only slight modifications, they themselves were used for worship. To the round centralised area was added an apse at the East end, the iconostasis (see page 34) and a few ancillary rooms. The result was the kind of building we regard as typical of Eastern Orthodox churches. These round buildings contributed to a rather different atmosphere. It was not, however, entirely due to the influence of the architecture.

The division between the Eastern (Orthodox) church and the West was at first little more than the geographical distinction the labels suggest. It hardened only gradually over a number of centuries but the position was certainly aggravated during and after the reign of Constantine. The Emperor moved his capital eastwards from Rome to Byzantium, or Constantinople as it was later called, and after his death the empire which had been united under his rule was divided between his sons. Of much more significance were the doctrinal disagreements of the period. Before the Council of Nicaea, called together by Constantine in A.D. 325, these were largely confined to the East. Although Nicaea was a meeting for the whole church, very few Westerners attended. Later the situation developed into a quarrel between East and West, each at times championing one side of the argument. Doctrinal controversy soon became entangled with ecclesiastical politics, and there were times in the fourth century when the two wings of the church seemed on the verge of separation.

Although it was not yet to become a complete break, they continued to drift apart and this is reflected in the story of the Liturgy. The developing differences should not be exaggerated. The East had given a great deal to the West. They still had much in common, and the broad outline of the Liturgy is recognisably the same. It is obscured, particularly in the East, by the addition of prayers and litanies at several moments in the service said by the congregation and led by the deacon. They had the advantage of giving the laity much more to do but these added details make it more difficult to discern the essential core.

Although sharing a common inheritance the two ways of worship began to have lives of their own. The growing independence of the West was made plain when Latin took over from the traditional Greek of the East as the language of the Liturgy. But this was not the only difference.

In the West for example the service tended to vary rather more from one week to another. There was a certain amount of variety in the East where there was, and still is, more than one Liturgy. They do not differ greatly from each other. That of St. Chrysostom is most commonly used. It is a later and shortened version of the Liturgy of St. Basil. This is substituted on the eve of certain feasts, on most of the Sundays of Lent and the Thursday and Saturday of Holy Week. A third alternative is called the Liturgy of the Pre-Sanctified. It is used on days like Good Friday which are hardly festive enough for the Eucharist to be celebrated. There is no consecration of the bread and wine though people often receive bread and wine consecrated on an earlier occasion. Apart from these variations, Eastern worship gives a strong impression of doing and saying the same things over and over again.

Unlike the East, the West did not occasionally substitute one entire though similar Liturgy for another, but, using the same Liturgy, regularly changed certain parts of it. We are not now referring to the scriptural readings which changed in any case. The 'ordinary' of the Mass is that part of the service which remains the same Sunday after Sunday. The Prayer of Consecration or Canon of the Mass would come under this heading. A canon or rule refers to something which is fixed. The 'propers' on the other hand refer to the prayers which are appropriate to the special day or season of the year, so that the prayers for Easter could hardly be used for Christmas, whereas in the East the same prayers would have been equally suitable at any time. The way the calendar is allowed to influence the service, so that it is altered to fit the occasion, is a distinctive feature of the Western rite. It seems to take more notice of time, whereas the fixed ritual of the East is rather more aloof and concerned with what is unchanging and eternal. To take part in its Liturgy is to enter a timeless world.

One of the most striking features of the Eastern Orthodox church

33

building is the dividing screen which runs right across the front and completely blocks the view. It is known as the iconostasis. It is virtually a wall pierced by two smaller doors on either side and the main or Royal Doors in the centre. In front of the screen is the nave for the worshipping congregation, and behind it is the Bema, as the area is called, with the holy table in the centre and the bishop's throne behind. Amongst other things there is another table for the preparation of the elements during the rite called the Prothesis which precedes the main service.

In one sense the iconostasis does not represent a difference between East and West in that it probably originated in the growing fear of the sacramental bread and wine which became common to both. The elements were regarded as almost dangerous and best left to the clergy to handle. The laity may well have preferred this in their awesome dread, and the ecclesiastics no doubt encouraged it by marking off the area where the real action now took place from the area of the church open to the public.

There are different theories as to why these barriers, found in all churches, eventually grew higher in the East. The name 'iconostasis' means a stand for the pictures or icons which are so characteristic of Orthodox churches. These were hung on the low wall which separated the sanctuary and the nave. As they grew in number, representing the saints and the holy family, so the wall grew in height to accommodate them all. Alternatively the wall, with its three doors, may be inspired by the stage design of Greek theatres, an appropriate setting for such a dramatic presentation of the Liturgy. A third possibility is that the iconostasis shows the influence of the Jewish synagogue where the scrolls were kept behind a dividing partition.

At first sight then, the barrier appears to be more complete in the East than in the West, but the opposite is in fact the case. Unlike the West there was a good deal of coming and going from one side of the screen to the other. At the Little Entrance, for example, when the Gospel is about to be read, the side doors are opened and the Gospel is carried out into the midst of the congregation with a good deal of ceremony. Again, at the Great Entrance, there is an even more impressive procession when the bread and wine are carried out of the side doors, through the worshipping people and into the Royal Doors, to be laid on the holy table as Christ was laid in the tomb. The deacon, who leads the people in the various litanies, is also a kind of go-between linking the people in the nave and the events in the sanctuary.

The two parts of the church do not therefore remain entirely separate as in the West, but the one invades the other. If in the loosely defined ideas of the East the area behind the screen is associated with the heavenly realm and eternal life, and the nave with man's mortal existence in this world, then the traffic between the two suggests in a dramatic way the gracious descent of the one to the other, the mysterious mingling of the two and the presence of God with man. If the West aspires to a distant, transcendent God, the East welcomes the God who comes amongst his people.

Turning to another noticeable difference between the worship of East and West, perhaps the most impressive moment of the Western rite, certainly as it developed in the Middle Ages, was the elevation of the host, when the consecrated elements were lifted up in full view of the congregation and a bell was rung to indicate that the moment had arrived with all its psychological power. It became of such importance that people talked of going to see the Mass! All attention was focused on the body and blood of Christ crucified for man's salvation.

This concentration on the cross cast a certain sadness and solemnity on the service. A further reminder of what it was mainly about was the great Rood or realistic reproduction of Christ on his cross which dominated the screen at the front of the church which separated the sanctuary and the nave. As the people looked towards the altar they could not help but see the dying Jesus.

The East was far from forgetting the suffering and death of the Lord, but neither did it forget his Incarnation and Resurrection. As a result there is a note of joy and celebration in its worship which is missing from the Western rite. If the elevation of the host was an unforgettable moment in the West, there is an equally unforgettable moment in the East. The Royal Doors are flung open once again, and the elements are now carried out for the communion of the people, symbolising the Resurrection of Christ. One commentator has noted how one of the Eastern rites alters the familiar words of Scripture, bending them to its instinctive mood:

> "For as often as ye eat this bread and drink this cup, ye
> do proclaim the death of the Son of Man *and confess*
> *His Resurrection* until He comes."

One other important difference should be mentioned before we look at the thinking behind them all. It is found in the great prayer of thanksgiving, the second of the four actions of the Eucharist. The prayer, sometimes called the Anaphora in the East, includes (see page 7) thanksgiving for all God's goodness, the words of Institution, a memorial of the Passion and Resurrection of Christ (Anamnesis) and the Epiklesis, a prayer which asks for the presence and blessing of the Holy Spirit. The point to notice is the moment of consecration when the bread and wine which have been brought at the offertory are set apart for their special use in the Eucharist as the body and blood of Christ. In the West this happens at the Institution. The repetition of the words of Jesus: "This is my body" transforms the bread into the consecrated host and in a similar way the words: "This cup is the new covenant sealed by my blood" transforms the wine. In the East the bread and wine are consecrated at the Epiklesis when the priest prays for the Holy Spirit to descend and change them into the body and blood of Christ, the food of his people and the pledge of their immortality.

We have briefly noted some of the more obvious differences between East and West as their ways of worship gradually grew apart without becoming entirely distinct. In the East there is a sense of timelessness, whereas the greater influence of the calendar on the Liturgy of the West makes the worshipper more aware of living in the changing times and seasons of this world. In the East the people are caught up into that eternal realm which graciously comes down among them, dramatically portrayed by impressive forays from the sanctuary behind the iconostasis into the main body of the church. This idea is also suggested by other features of the service. In the West, there is a single-minded concentration on the death of Christ, whereas the East, without forgetting the Passion, is more consciously aware of the Incarnation and Resurrection of Christ. Finally we noted that the bread and wine are consecrated at the Institution in the West and the Epiklesis in the East.

Without trying to make things too neat and tidy, some light can be shed on all these differences by remembering that behind them are two rather different ideas about salvation, what it is, and how God has made it possible for men through Christ. We may not find either of them wholly satisfying today but they were meaningful at the time.

In the West the problem is seen in terms of man's sinful disobedience against God and the need to restore good relations between the two. Justice demands punishment but salvation is achieved by the sacrifice of Christ for the sins of the world. That is why the thought of it everywhere dominates the Mass and attention is concentrated almost exclusively on the Passion. The climax comes when the consecrated elements, the body and blood of our Lord, are offered afresh, and the sacrifice is re-presented before the eyes of the people as it is before God. To the more legally minded West it was of vital importance that the sacrifice was valid. The only satisfying evidence was that of our Lord himself; so the consecration was appropriately associated with the Institution narrative and his own words which gave dominical authority to what the church was doing.

This idea of the sacrifice of the Mass has given rise to a good deal of debate from time to time, and it caused offence when crude and mistaken ideas became widespread. That does not mean that there were not and are not other, more acceptable interpretations. But the point for us to notice is that behind many of the distinctive features of the Western Liturgy lies this idea of Christ our Redeemer offering the sacrifice for sin and here and now opening up the way to God. The Agnus Dei expresses succinctly the focus of attention in the West, though interestingly enough it was imported from the East at the end of the seventh century by Pope Sergius, reminding us not to make the separation of East and West too absolute or too soon. As the bread is broken and again shown to the people, the prayer of the priest strikes the central note of adoration:

"O Lamb of God that takest away the sins of the world,
have mercy upon us."

In the East, the problem has to do with corruptible human nature and the fact that man is mortal and will die. Salvation is not so much the forgiveness of sins as the gift of life which is both eternal and divine. It is achieved by the gracious humility of God who through his son Jesus Christ enters this mortal realm at his Incarnation and even its corruption and death at his crucifixion and burial. In so doing however he infects the human with the divine, the corruptible with the incorruptible, and by his Resurrection and Ascension lifts man up from the temporal into the eternal sphere. The Eastern view is typified by this prayer of adoration:

"Being true life, O Christ, Thou as a God of compassion didst garb Thyself with my corrupt nature, and didst descend into the dust of death, O Master, and didst rend mortality asunder, and rising on the third day didst clothe dead bodies with incorruption."

37

Against this background we can understand why the consecration comes at the Epiklesis. It is not the moment when the validity of the sacrifice is seen to rest on Christ's own words, but the moment at which the Holy Spirit descends upon the gifts of bread and wine; the things of this world, including man himself, being sanctified by the coming of the divine life. So changed, the elements become not so much the sacrifice of Christ to be offered but the food of our immortality. It is the words of John rather than Paul which come to mind:

> "In truth, in very truth I tell you, unless you eat the flesh of the Son of Man and drink his blood you can have no life in you. Whoever eats my flesh and drinks my blood possesses eternal life, and I will raise him up on the last day." (John 6.53 f.)

Associated ideas of Christ coming to where we are in order to bring us to where he is, and of becoming like us that we might become like him, explain why the whole Story is important to the East rather than a narrower preoccupation with Christ's suffering and death. Our salvation is to be caught up in the saga of the descent of Christ to man that man might ascend with Christ to God.

The suggested mingling of heaven and earth in the Liturgy, the way it tends to turn its back on time and the welcome given to God as he comes among his people are all of a piece. They offer the worshipper a foretaste of his salvation as he enters for a while the realm of eternal life. If to go to the Western rite is to go to the sacrifice and be released from the wages of sin, to go to the Eastern rite is to take part in a mystery by which man is rescued from his finitude and the world is permeated with the divine life.

Here then are two very different theologies, or accounts of what God has done for us in Christ. To discover how they arose would require a complicated though fascinating piece of investigation. Right from the start people were not content merely to tell the Story. If we emphasised this idea in the previous chapter (see page 16 ff.) as a way of understanding what we are doing basically at the Liturgy, no one suggests that we can stop there.

We cannot stop at telling the Story and rehearsing the events concerning Jesus of Nazareth because we want to know what it all means. It is doubtful in fact that we can talk about 'events' at all without interpreting them to a certain extent. From the start the early Christians, upon whom these events made such an overwhelming impression, tried to put their significance into words and express something of what this revealing Story had to tell them about God and themselves, life and death, good and evil, the past and the future, and the realities of their experience. It was a battle of words in so far as they had to fight to find any words that would do and found themselves stretching language to its limits, but speak they must about what had happened and what it now meant to them.

These interpretations of the Story influenced the Liturgy as we have tried to show, but in saying this two qualifications should be made. First, we are not suggesting that where a feature of worship reflects a particular theology it is the only influence at work. In some cases this is so. One could think of some examples from the Reformation period, such as the removal of references to the sacrifice of the Mass, where there is a direct and simple line from theological convictions to changes made in worship; but it would be foolish to suggest, for example, that theology is the only reason why the consecration comes at a different moment in the East than in the West, or that the only reason why the East did not allow the calendar to give rise to variable prayers in worship was because it thought of salvation in terms of a changeless eternity rather than the redemption of time. Theology is only one factor amongst many.

Second, no one suggests that theology influences worship in the sense that someone first sat down and worked out the correct theory or theological blue-print from which the actual practical details of the Liturgy were then read off. Worship, as we have already noted, in the form of the early meals and the meetings for preaching and fellowship and the prayers, was there from the start. It was prior to theological reflection. There is a real parallel here between the Liturgy and the actual events concerning Jesus. Worship already existed. The events had already taken place. The Liturgy was being performed. The Story was being told. Both gave rise to various theologies or attempts to put the significance of it all into words. In turn these theologies or interpretations doubled back as it were and affected the way the Story was told and the way the Liturgy was performed. As a result, the Gospels, especially the first three, which many have thought of as giving us more or less the plain facts about Jesus, tell the Story in a certain way. They are not clinically detached accounts of what happened, even if such accounts were possible, but the events seen now through the interpretative eyes of the early church which had begun to think seriously about the meaning of all that had happened. These interpretations are not to be suspected as mischievous. They do not mislead us but usually enrich our understanding of Jesus. When we tell the Story today by reading the Gospels for example, we do not start with the events but with a theologically coloured account of the events, and if those events, though recognisably the same, look rather different as we read the four evangelists, it is partly because their theologies were not identical.

In a similar way, the Liturgy is not the direct product of theology, but the theologies it inspired had a real effect, and in so far as they varied they contributed to variety in ways of worship.

Bearing in mind these qualifications, we can say that some features of worship, and some of the differences between one Liturgy and another, are there for theological reasons.

Differences of temperament

After the seventh century the Eastern rite did not change or develop a very great deal. Its very understanding of the Story it told turned its eyes to an eternal and changeless world which prejudiced it against significant variation.

In the West however the tale is rather more complicated, and there is much more variety. The Liturgies which grew up are usually divided into two main groups, namely the Italian rites, the most important of which were the rites of the church in Rome, and the Gallican rites, which is a loose way of referring to the many others such as those of Spain (Mozarabic) and Britain (Celtic), but in particular those of ancient Gaul. The origin of the Gallican rites is uncertain, though the influence of the East is fairly marked. At the time no one thought in terms of Gallican and Roman rites of course. These were no more than local variations on one liturgical theme, variations which tended to harden into real differences when communications were made more difficult, for example, by the disorder which followed the decline of the Roman Empire.

By the time we pick up the story again in the second half of the eighth century it was a very varied picture indeed. Some have described it as being more like ecclesiastical anarchy. Certainly the church was badly disorganised, ignorant and corrupt. It had been through dark days.

The Frankish king, Pepin the Short, made an attempt to sort things out round about 760, but the main credit has usually been given to his son, Charlemagne, who succeeded his father in 768. He became sole ruler on the death of his brother in 771 and was crowned as the first Holy Roman Emperor on Christmas Day 800 by Pope Leo III.

Charlemagne showed vigour as a ruler not only by successful conquests abroad but also by the renewed order and consistency which he brought to many areas of civil and ecclesiastical life at home. His tidy mind tried to bring greater uniformity to the church's worship, and in this and other reforms he was helped by Alcuin, an English scholar and monk educated at the cathedral school in York.

The basis for the reformed Liturgy which Charlemagne wished all parts of the church to adopt was to be a revision of the Roman rite attributed to Pope Gregory in the sixth century and known as the Gregorian Sacramentary. Charlemagne turned to it for more than one reason. He acted partly out of political astuteness since at the time his eyes were on Rome and its inclusion in his empire as the culmination of his territorial ambitions.

But fortunately for him this Roman rite had already crossed the Alps and was widely used in Gaul. It was similar to many other rites in that it was no more than a local variation of the basic Liturgy common to all. Succeeding Popes had specifically disclaimed any imperialistic ambitions to make it the norm and impose it on non-Roman churches. Nevertheless its influence had gradually made itself felt. The advice of Rome was often sought, and when enquiries concerned liturgical matters the most straightforward way of dealing with them was to send copies of the Roman rite and suggest that here was a good example to follow, which they did, combining it with some of their own Gallican material. The earlier Gelasian Sacramentary which originally dates from the fifth century but later circulated in Gaul in other forms is an example of this. As a result, to take the Roman rite as a basis for an official Liturgy did not mean imposing something entirely unknown. It existed however in many editions, since over the years Rome's advice had been taken in different ways. By now it was difficult to tell the original material from the rest, so Charlemagne asked the Pope (Hadrian I) for a standard text. In reply he received what appears to have been a very inadequate and incomplete book, with a lot of empty spaces. It contained no instructions for any of the ordinary Sundays of the year—which meant the majority—and only dealt with the great festivals and special occasions.

This was one reason why Alcuin had to get to work, but in his wisdom he was well aware of another perhaps more pressing reason for editing and enlarging this Gregorian Sacramentary sent from Rome if it was ever to become the 'book of common prayer' for the whole of the Western church.

Knowing the Frankish people he was dealing with, he knew that they would not take kindly to the Roman way of worship purged of all that had gradually been combined with it over the years. They might respect it, but they would not like it, not because they disagreed with its underlying ideas but because Rome's way of doing things could never be theirs. It was a matter of temperament, not theology, and it stands out fairly clearly when we compare Roman and Gallican material.

The differences are not all of one kind. Some are clearly due to historical circumstances. Take the prayers. Gallican prayers bear many of the marks of the Dark Ages, with its barbarism, turmoil and brutality. The picture which results is a rather negative one of endless battles against evil and the yearning for rest (requiem) and security in a world which appeared to lack both.

The most significant difference is not so much the content however, as the general style. This can be illustrated with reference to the collect, a type of prayer still much admired. It is often used as a way of summing up or collecting the prayers of the congregation after a period of silence, and this usage may well have given it its name. Many fine examples were composed by Thomas Cranmer, Archbishop of Canterbury, who was largely responsible for the English prayer book of 1552; but the collect is much older than that. It is one of the distinctive contributions of the West to Christian worship. Whilst not exclusive to Rome, it is in Rome that it appears to have flourished, and in Roman books such as the Gregorian Sacramentary it came to fine expression, as if there the collect felt more at home than anywhere else.

Almost by definition it was brief and to the point. It was usually content to say one thing and to leave it at that. It was a finely balanced literary composition with no wasted words. It was not entirely cold, but it was restrained. Percy Dearmer once described it as "an epigram softened by feeling". Here is an example:

> O Lord, we beseech thee mercifully to receive the prayers of thy people which call upon thee; and grant that they may both perceive and know what things they ought to do, and also may have grace and power faithfully to fulfil the same; through Jesus Christ our Lord.

In many ways the collect is typical of the Roman rite as a whole. Words like 'straightforward', 'business-like' and 'reserved' come to mind. There are no frills or emotional scenes. It is simple to the point of being prosaic. We can discern the same cast of mind as that which preferred the tidy legal transactions of the sacrifice to the vaguer Eastern mysteries of divinisation when it came to putting the significance of the Story into words.

In contrast the Gallican rites were much longer. Words flowed and phrase was piled upon phrase. Language bordered on the verbose but it expressed a wealth of human affection and emotional warmth. The same temperament was reflected throughout a more sensuous Liturgy which had more colour and much more room for ceremonial than the less flamboyant Roman rite.

The root of these differences is the root cause of variety in general within the Western tradition at the time, and that is the temperament of the people concerned, in this case the sober-minded Roman on the one hand and the more extrovert Franks on the other.

Alcuin was wise enough to know that if he completely replaced the existing Gallican rites, already influenced by Roman advice, by the rite he found in the Gregorian Sacramentary sent from Rome to Charlemagne he would be courting disaster. Many would regard it as cramping their style. The problem was solved by dividing the new book into two halves. In the first was Alcuin's completed version of the Gregorian rite. In the second, a 'supplement', was a great deal of material from Gallican sources.

The original intention was to make the first part compulsory and the second an optional extra. This was the official position, and once the new service book was complete all Gallican rites were suppressed. In practice however the distinction between the two halves of the book was gradually eroded. More and more of the supplementary Gallican material was introduced into the authorised Liturgy and eventually it was incorporated on a more or less permanent basis as an integral part of the rite itself.

The final result was not the conquest of the Gallican rites by the Roman rite but mutual co-existence, and it was this mixture or synthesis of the two which became the basis for the Western Mass which has come down to us by way of the Roman Catholic Church. It has within it two devotional moods and it is worth remembering that many of the features which are dubbed as 'Romanising', such as bell-ringing, censing, genuflexion and a good deal of ceremonial, are not really the responsibility of sober old Rome at all, but are part of the legacy of the Gallican rites.

43

Three comments

Our main reason for looking at one or two chapters of the story of the Liturgy from Constantine to Charlemagne was to illustrate how variety in worship can be traced back to historical circumstances, theological ideas and the temperaments of the worshippers. Without suggesting that this is an exhaustive list, three comments may be made in conclusion.

a) When we are discussing a particular feature of the Liturgy or the form and content of worship in general, whether to criticise and reform it or to justify and keep it as it is, it is useful to recognise these historical, theological and temperamental factors for what they are. They cannot be entirely separated but it is helpful to make distinctions. If we realise, for example, that a certain aspect of worship is the result of an historical accident and does not involve any great matter of principle it can take some of the steam out of the argument. If it fails to do so we shall see more clearly that we are dealing with an area in which people feel very deeply and that something more than rational argument will be required if creative change is to take place. To see things for what they are can also give us a sense of perspective, and enable us to avoid giving a permanent place to what is of only temporary value. In the case of temperamental factors in worship, it can save us from imposing on everyone what may only be appropriate for a few. Let us take two examples in a little more detail. One has to do with forms of worship and the other with the plea for more physical and emotional rather than intellectual activity.

In Free Church circles there can still be found a deeply ingrained suspicion of what are referred to as 'liturgical' or set forms of worship. It finds expression in a dislike of Anglican services, often the only other form of worship known from experience, and a general uneasiness about the use of prayer books and written congregational material. Little importance is attached to the right ordering of worship. Liturgy tends to be a dirty word. It is not used as we are using it to denote the characteristic act of Christian worship, but as if it inevitably implied rigid procedures where everything is written down for constant repetition and no room is left for freedom or variety.

There are many reasons for this suspicion. For one thing, a significant number of Christians in England trace their ancestry back to the Separatists of the sixteenth century who looked for a radical reformation of the church more thoroughgoing than what they regarded as the half-hearted compromise of the Elizabethan Settlement in 1559. They were too impatient to work for reform from within and separated from the church to form independent congregations of their own. Amongst these groups there was radical opposition to all set forms of worship which arose out of a passionate belief in the unfettered working of the Holy Spirit. This was often understood in terms of immediate inspiration so that nothing must hinder its promptings. "Where the Spirit of the Lord is, there is liberty" (2 Cor. 3.17). Written prayer was no prayer at all, and setting it to music in the form of hymns did not make it any better! Even sermons prepared before the service were frowned on. Only extempore preaching could be an adequate vehicle for the spontaneous and unexpected activity of the Spirit.

Here then are objections which have to do with theological convictions. They are matters of principle. Of a rather different sort are the arguments against fixed and repetitious patterns of worship that appear to be little more than common sense. They point out for instance that if you keep on saying the same things there is the danger of becoming rather mechanical. Those who actually do say the same things do not feel as mechanised as they are said to appear and can suggest some advantages on the other side. Mechanical repetition can discipline the mind, concentrating it and setting it remarkably free for its devotions. Furthermore, if the service is provided for you, at least you are not entirely at the mercy of an ungifted or ill-prepared leader or subject to his moods or personal inclinations.

On the whole the argument over whether worship should be fixed or free is a non-issue as long as it is seen in terms of 'both/and' not in terms of 'either/or'. We have argued that there is a fixed element round which there is plenty of room to move. Such a concern for properly ordered worship does not necessarily insist on having everything fixed and final, and so-called free worship for that matter can become as routine and predictable as prescribed services.

The use of written material is in many ways no more than a tool which enables the congregation to join in. It does not preclude individual and even extempore contributions, and it does not mean that the same written material must be used all the time.

All forms of worship can run into trouble, but here it is not so much a question of principle as of balance and proportion. There is room for different emphases but all of them must be kept in check.

But if the position can be stated so sensibly, why is it that prejudice still takes over at times, so that reasoned discussion and even theological argument give way to hardened opposition? It is unwise to trace cause and effect too confidently, but this prejudice against forms may well owe more to the history of the Puritans than to the principles of the Separatists.

Puritanism was, strictly speaking, a movement for church reform which began in the middle of the sixteenth century and came to an end in 1662. The Puritans or purifiers were also disappointed with the Elizabethan Settlement of Religion after the severe persecutions under Mary. Things improved but they did not go far enough. Unlike the Separatists, the Puritans were prepared to attack the status quo from the inside rather than the outside. They had their heyday in the Commonwealth Period (1649-1658) but after the death of Cromwell and the restoration of the monarchy they fell into decline and unpopularity.

In matters of worship the Puritans were not opposed to liturgical forms. Greatly influenced by the continental reformers, especially Calvin, service books originating in Geneva were widely used. Their Westminster Directory of 1644 certainly went no further than making suggestions to ministers about how best to conduct the services, but the famous Puritan, Richard Baxter, actually submitted a Reformed Liturgy to the Savoy Conference in 1661, in an attempt to win concessions for the Puritan cause.

They were not therefore against liturgical forms on principle, but the Puritans were opposed to one particular liturgical form, and that was the Book of Common Prayer, mainly because of its contents and the way it was forced upon everyone whether they agreed with it or not.

Elizabeth re-issued it in 1559 as part of her measures to keep an already difficult peace. To Puritan eyes the book showed too great an affinity with Rome and too little zeal for reformation according to the Word of God. It reminded them of unbiblical practices which they detested and a doctrine of transubstantiation which they disowned. Puritan policies were increasingly hammered out in the context of violent opposition.

Matters came to a head soon after the Savoy Conference of 1661 at which the Book of Common Prayer was reviewed and the Puritans hoped to gain concessions with the help of Richard Baxter's proposals. They were not successful and only trivial alterations were subsequently made. Virtually the same old book was imposed on the church by the Act of Uniformity in 1662. Many could not accept it and two thousand Puritans who refused to conform were deprived of their livings in the Great Ejection which followed.

Inevitably these non-conformists were driven into much closer relations with the more radical Separatists whose theology may have strengthened their own antagonisms. Their dislike of one particular set form now escalated into a prejudice against them all. If that prejudice still exists and to some extent is a focus of differences between two traditions of worship in England, it is well to realise that it does not rest entirely on matters of principle.

The 1662 book can be criticised for its inflexibility, and good arguments can be advanced for more room to manoeuvre. It is not all prejudice, but if events had turned out differently and had not provoked the kind of reaction which they did, the debate about forms of worship might not have been conducted in such absolute terms. Victims of circumstance became men of principle. Extreme protests, appropriate for the time being, became permanently held convictions. Defensive positions were taken up under pressure. Where they are perpetuated they may represent little more than a painful hangover from a largely forgotten past.

To turn to a second illustration of the importance of recognising an issue for what it is, there is increasing criticism of ways of worship which rely almost exclusively on verbal communication, make their appeal to the intellect, and are reserved to the point of being inhibited. The critics wish to enrich if not to replace them with liturgies which allow greater opportunity for tactile experience, movement and dance, and a greater degree of emotional exhuberance. Pentecostalism has much to contribute in this respect and its growing influence across denominational frontiers indicates that its contribution is not necessarily wedded to one particular doctrinal point of view.

More than one issue is raised by this growing appreciation of what one might label the 'physical' and 'emotional' as distinct from the 'cerebral', and we shall return to some of them later in our discussion of multi-media worship. Here we shall only refer briefly to one, without implying that it can be entirely separated from the rest. If it is not always possible to deal with one thing at a time we ought at least to distinguish between different things since greater clarity can often contribute to a more adequate response.

There are many good reasons for moving away from our rather polite and staid services, and most people will welcome the move to some extent, but we should be sensitive to the fact that it is partly a matter of temperament. This may save us from making another error instead of correcting a mistake. The mistake has sometimes been to assume that everyone is equally capable of coping with a rather intellectual approach to worship. Even though we are often quick to assert that you do not have to be clever to be a Christian, we tend to assume that Christians are by nature dealers in words and abstract ideas.

If this is now seen to be untrue, it would be unfortunate if it were to be replaced by the equally doctrinaire assumption that everyone should feel free to dance and openly express their feelings in worship. No doubt many of us who suppress whole areas of our personalities should find a greater freedom for our own good, and may well do so in time. Others maybe never will, and they should not feel excluded from the Liturgy if they are unable to do so, anymore than it should exclude the non-intellectual if only by implication. Different types of people are involved and they operate most successfully in different ways. Whereas we should insist that at the Liturgy they should tell the Story and celebrate the Eucharist we must avoid insisting that they should all do so in pentecostal style anymore than in the best traditions of the English gentleman. It is in part the difference between the Gallican and Roman rites all over again and we should respect it as much as the wise monk Alcuin respected it in the age of Charlemagne.

It would be a pity if a proper sensitivity in this matter were allowed to bolster up the familiar argument in favour of Christian disunity, that we need different churches to provide different types of worship in order to cater for different types of people. We certainly need variety and are hardly likely to avoid it, but we also need Liturgies that are inclusive of all sorts and conditions of men and enable Christians to be all together in one place. We must not typecast the faith but allow the intellect, the body and the feelings to find expression, if not in every individual then in the corporate activity as a whole. We must do so however with sufficient imagination to avoid the fear that can be aroused by emotional coercion and the inferiority that can be induced by intellectual imperialism, and the Liturgy must foster the courtesy which leaves the worshipper free to sit this one out or to join in the dance.

b) Having enquired into the factors which give rise to any particular feature of the Liturgy, we should be open to the possibility that should any one of them no longer hold good then its effect on the Liturgy is no longer legitimate.

A certain style of worship for example is not necessarily normative nor intrinsically Christian, just as the faith itself is not intrinsically bound up with the traditions of European civilisation. In a different civilisation it must be allowed to take on a different shape. Once the Liturgy moves out of a particular ethos then the style which it fostered may have to be abandoned. The point seems obvious once made, but it is too often obscured by unquestioned assumptions.

In many areas, for example, the multi-racial society is now becoming a reality, and in most cases this will mean for the church an encounter with other faiths and nothing so simple as coming to terms with Christians drawn from cultural backgrounds different from our own. Where it does mean that, however, we must not assume that the way forward is to educate the newcomers into our way of doing things. Where this has happened, and other approaches to worship have been suppressed, the newcomers have not unreasonably been disappointed and some have hived off to worship on their own. That is not the way forward either. The creative task is a long and difficult one. It may well involve at first the fostering of distinctive traditions, but not in isolation from each other, in the hope that all will gradually be enriched, and as far as the Liturgy is concerned, that styles will emerge which do not obstinately perpetuate a sectarian approach but bear some relation to the diversified culture in terms of which it must now be done.

Similar questions should be asked in relation to different social as well as racial groups. We have become aware, in recent years, of the suburban captivity of the churches. With notable exceptions, which include the Roman Catholic community, the institutional church finds much of the strength that remains to it in middle-class, private housing estates. Attempts to transplant it into other areas, whether residential or non-residential, are too often seen as trying to build the same kind of churches reproducing the same patterns, usually because it has not occurred to us that there are others. Styles of worship have been imprisoned in this captivity along with other aspects of church life. We must recognise how relative they are, and ask if an industrial worker, for example, has any obligation whatsoever to conform to what may seem perfectly natural to suburban man but which gives him the definite feeling of not being himself.

We are gradually learning our lesson in other respects and we do not need to labour the point. The phrase 'church music' can properly refer to music played and sung in churches, but it must not imply that only music of a certain period or of sufficient antiquity has the proper credentials for use in worship. The music of Bach and the Victorians has contributed much to worship in the past. Some of it is still appreciated and is judged by uncertain canons of taste to have more lasting value. We cannot assume however, and fortunately do not do so, that it has any claim to a monopoly; and if it owes much to one period it may have less to contribute to another. Similarly, the language of King James and the Authorised Version may still give aesthetic pleasure, but it is as outdated and archaic as the Latin of the Mass, and neither should be confused with the language of Zion.

We must be aware of this possibility of change not only where aspects of the Liturgy are relative to cultural factors, but also where they are relative to historical circumstances. It would be interesting to compare our own age with the age of Constantine referred to earlier in this chapter. In some ways the position is reversed. That is not to suggest that the church which was freed from persecution in the fourth century is now being subjected to it once again, at least not within the experience of most of us. Christians who talk in such terms are prone to a rather perverse evaluation of our comparative comfort. It would be better to take a hard-headed look at what has to be done in a secular age than to lapse into any martyr complex.

No, we are not subjected to persecution, but in other ways we may look more like the pre-Nicene church than the church after the Emperor gave it peace. Once again the church is a minority group. It does not enjoy even the nominal allegiance of the majority. Once again the church represents one religion amongst many in a pluralist society. In both these senses we, like the early Christians, do not live in a Christendom situation where church and society become virtually all of a piece. If under Constantine the church became 'established' in all but name, now it is little more than the name which is left. The concern for and involvement with the whole national life, which establishment represents for some, is admirable, but it is hardly realistic to regard Christianity as the religion of the state.

This change of circumstances, not to say reversal of fortunes, might lead us to question the assumptions behind such a phrase as 'Public Worship'. It can mean more than one thing. To abandon it is not to suggest that worship should cease to be out in the open and once again hide itself away. It was hidden away largely for fear of the consequences if the authorities found out what was taking place. There is no need for that kind of secrecy. Nor are we referring here to the theological point that the Liturgy should not be public, as indeed it should not, because it is the distinctive activity of those who are committed to telling the Story. The *disciplina arcani* or 'secret discipline' of the early Christians may have been strengthened for security reasons, but it rested on the understanding that the Liturgy was the business of the Christian community and was not for the public at large. It became public when, in later centuries, there was technically no one to exclude, because all were baptised. Clearly this is not so now, and we should avoid the practice of bringing all and sundry to the Liturgy. It is not for them. But this is a matter of principle rather than of historical circumstance.

When worship became public in the fourth century there was more to it than the end of secretive meetings and the need to exclude non-Christians from the central Christian rite. Worship also went public in another sense by moving into public buildings and holding services not for small groups but for large numbers of people. The buildings and the numbers involved had notable effects on the kind of activity which then took place. Participation declined and worship became less intimate and more formal.

When we now find, as we frequently do, much smaller groups of people still meeting in large public buildings and observing the same curious formality, it is time to ask whether circumstances alter cases. Where Christians again become a minority group is it time for their worship to move out of the public eye and become more private, informal and participatory, finding a style of meeting which is both more intense and more modest and also more appropriate for those who tell their Story against the spirit of the age?

These comments refer to the Liturgy. They do not deny a place to public and even large scale attempts to communicate the Gospel. Neither need we totally exclude more impressive but occasional acts of worship where small Christian groups gather together for their festivals in cathedral-like buildings, so gaining an energising experience of the great church. So often we fall between two stools. Small groups meeting in cathedral-like settings are only made aware of their dwindling size which is hardly the point of meeting. At the same time they deny themselves all the advantages to be gained by foregoing the trappings of public worship for the possibilities of more intimate occasions. The developments of the fourth century have been described as 'from house-church to church-house'. Changed historical circumstances suggest that we might retrace our steps.

The general point is that certain features of the Liturgy should be open to change if the factors out of which they arose no longer hold good. This may not be hard to accept where cultural influences and historical circumstances are concerned. It is rather harder when we turn to theology, mainly because we feel that here we ought to be on more permanent ground. Talking about theology seems more like talking about the principle of a thing, and we stand by our principles, we do not alter them. That is true, and we ought to stand by our convictions, though without that nervous defensiveness which is not prepared to re-examine them from time to time. We must also refuse to compromise our beliefs merely to make them more acceptable to those who do not agree.

In what sense then could a theology no longer hold good so that we need to reconsider the validity of those aspects of worship which appear to depend on it?

Perhaps the short answer is that theology does change whether we like it or not and since it subsequently influences our worship, that is likely to change as well. Our pictures of God have changed for example from thinking of him as being 'out there' in a supernatural realm quite apart from our own, though occasionally paying us a visit, to a view of him as being 'in here', still different from us but not so distant as we had grown to imagine. He is God with us, all the time, as part of the very texture of our world and our lives. Some have seen very direct consequences of that for worship. We must return to them later, but as far as the arrangements for the Liturgy are concerned, the long basilican-style building with the altar-table way up at the front and its whole sense of direction moving forwards and often upwards away from the worshippers is too suggestive of a distant God. The round building with the table in the middle of the congregation focuses attention elsewhere and is more suggestive of the God who is found amongst his people.

There is a difference however between saying that theology does change and saying that it almost has to change, not merely to correct ideas that were wrong or to rediscover neglected aspects of Christian truth.

We can briefly illustrate why theology needs to change by remembering that if historical circumstances and cultural and temperamental factors contribute to the character of the Liturgy, they also contribute to the character of the theologies which influence our worship. In the case of historical circumstances, it is notable that pessimistic theologies often arise in dark times and more optimistic ones when times are brighter. To be influenced in this way may be judged a mistake, but other influences are not so open to criticism.

If theology is the attempt to put the significance of the events concerning Jesus into words, it is always made by particular people who are children of their time. They have peculiar characteristics. They think in a certain way. They use the images and intellectual tools that are to hand. Take the two theologies we spoke of earlier, one finding its home in the East and the other in the Western church. We have already hinted that the differences between them tell us a good deal about the characteristics of the people concerned as well as a good deal about Christ! The rather tidy theory of sacrifice whereby at the cross the price of man's sin is paid and the legal transaction is satisfactorily completed, is well suited to the more precise Roman mind, whereas the East, which did not care so much for definitions, was more hospitable to the vaguer mystery of God's coming amongst men and the divinisation of human life. Again the pictures and concepts they used to give body to the realities they had discerned in Christ were not wholly created by the Story but were harvested from ideas which were current in their day. The theology which results is like all theology. It is our response to the Christ; a mixture of the truth he reveals and the kind of people that we happen to be.

Theologies are never true in the sense that they are descriptions of objective realities with which any reasonable person looking at the same realities and living in any time or place would be bound to agree. There was no 'sacrifice' to be seen, only an execution which many people found it meaningful to think of in terms of sacrifice. There was no grand descent of the eternal world into the temporal sphere to rescue men from their mortality, but a human life of extraordinary quality which other people of a different cast of mind began to talk about in terms of an Incarnation of God. Their theologies, or attempts to talk about the meaning of the events, were carefully related to the events. They witnessed to the truth as they believed they had seen it in Jesus. They made every attempt to do him justice. But they did it in their way. Their way is not entirely ours. Whereas Jesus remains the same, a theology is never true for all time but only for those who make it up and for as long as others find it meaningful and are able to talk the same language and use the same pictures and forms of thought. In so far as these cultural factors change, the theology to which they helped to give expression will also change. If for example we do not wish to express the significance of Jesus either in terms of sacrifice in the technical sense or in terms of infecting mortal man with immortality, it does not mean that we wish to betray the faith or avoid its demands. It means

53

that times have changed and we must make our own attempt on our own terms to talk about the significance of the Story we are committed to tell.

But a changed way of understanding the Story may have implications for the Liturgy where it is told. Ways of worship may become inappropriate if they no longer adequately reflect what we have come to believe. The result is not necessarily to discard all the hymns and prayers, for example, which no longer put matters as we would wish to put them. With a little imagination we can still use them and honour them as expressions of faith valid for their time and by no means completely invalid for ours. They can still point us to the Christ. Neither is the result limited to writing contemporary hymns and prayers to supplement or replace the old ones, important as that may be. There are further consequences and we must look at them when we come to talk about the relevance of worship.

c) Finally, once we understand a little more about why things are as they are and have become open to the possibility of change, how do we sort out the wheat from the chaff? Whether we are looking back and trying to evaluate what we have received, or looking forward in an attempt to devise more satisfactory ways of worship for the future, where are the tools for a critique of the Liturgy? How in the end do we justify what we do?

This is a complicated question and we can only deal with it here in a somewhat superficial way. There are no straightforward authoritarian answers as to what is right in worship obtainable from either the Bible or the church. We should probably reject the idea that there is any view at all about worship, or about Christian belief and behaviour for that matter, which can claim to be absolutely right and beyond further discussion. That way of solving problems has always had its attractions but it can savour more of childish insecurity than pious obedience.

Freed from a false quest after final solutions and well aware that man must always live with tentative answers and partial insights, there are a number of available resources which can help us to be wise. If we believe in a God who is everywhere at work we shall expect to gain insights from all kinds of people and places, but as Christians we shall look more carefully for guidance in at least three directions.

First we shall learn from the past and make use of the long experience of the church. Mistakes have been made which we need not make again. Lessons have been learnt from which we can now benefit. Certain things have persisted not merely out of prejudice or habit, but because they have proved their worth. The Christian tradition may look at times like so much conservatism, but it also contains a great deal of accumulated wisdom which we shall not lightly dismiss.

Second, we shall pay attention to the Bible, and in so far as it is read regularly and systematically in the Liturgy it provides a built-in check. As long as the basic pattern is observed, with its lessons from the Old Testament, the Epistles and the Gospels, worship must always live with the Story, and there is at least the possibility of the one raising doubts about or re-invigorating the other. The Bible is important not because it provides instructions but chiefly because it was written so close to the events. If we value any theology of any age as a testimony to Jesus of Nazareth, and ask of it what must Jesus have been like to make these men speak as they did, then we especially value the witnesses and theologians of the Bible, not because they are more inspired or better at it than anyone else, though some 'apocryphal' material was set aside, but mainly because they had such a close-up view. The New Testament is the most immediate response to Jesus that we have and as such it is of quite absorbing interest. It has the added advantage of being a written document whose contents have been fixed (in the Canon of Scripture) for a very long time. We can play about with its interpretation but we cannot tamper with the text.

Third, we shall not only learn from the past and pay attention to the Bible, we shall also take heed of one another. We shall be careful not to do battle over worship on too narrow a front. Individuals have their idiosyncracies. Groups tend to be exclusive. Understanding is always limited. Insights and inclinations need balancing. Mistakes need correcting. The whole church, with its many members and denominations, openly exchanging views and engaging in free but tough-minded debate about the Liturgy is more likely to make wise decisions in this as in many other matters than groups which isolate themselves from the one holy catholic church and create narrower traditions of their own.

Here then are three directions in which to look, so that when we go on to discuss topics of current interest, even if our purpose is not to treat them exhaustively, we shall keep our eyes on the wisdom gained by past experience as well as the opinions of our contemporaries, and we shall wonder how far any trend or emphasis is compatible with the Story and our understanding of its significance.

We know we cannot read off any ready-made answers. We know

that we must try to give reasons but the argument is never entirely rational. We realise that many other factors such as historical circumstances, background, culture and temperament influence what we do. Above all perhaps, we accept that there are no guarantees. The Christian community with its present fellowship, its traditions and its Story book is no proof against error. It provides a context in which we must do our thinking and where in the end, having sought all the available help, we must make up our own minds. We usually learn best by doing, and there is a profound sense in which it is more important for us as responsible human beings to make decisions than to get them absolutely right.

III

COUNTERPOINT

We have seen how different groups in the church from time to
time and for different reasons have been responsible for a variety of
ways of doing and understanding the one enduring Liturgy. In recent
years there have been moves to restore the old skeletal pattern of
Word and Sacrament, and it can be clearly discerned in a number of
experiments and proposals for liturgical revision (see pages 5–7).
But we also have particular emphases of our own. We too contribute
to variety. The results are not entirely novel, and in some cases they
are rediscoveries of strands which run deep in the Christian tradition.
They are however departures from a more recent past. We shall look
at three of them in turn under the following headings:

1 All-join-in
2 Multi-media
3 Down-to-earth

All-join-in
The growing weight of opinion in favour of the whole congregation actively participating in the Liturgy certainly looks like the
recovery of a feature of Christian worship at one time so characteristic as to be almost taken for granted. It is the lack of it that needs
explaining. Those in favour hardly need to justify themselves as
innovators!

It would be difficult to find in the records of the early church anything remotely like the clergy dominated performances, not to mention
one-man shows, that many have grown up to regard as the norm.

Descriptions of worship in the early days are few and far between
and we must not make too much of them, but what evidence we have
suggests that all joined in. In Corinth the enthusiasm of the congregation threatened chaos. Paul, in one of his letters, had to ask them
to wait their turn and speak one at a time, but he was far from dissuading them from taking part: "When you meet for worship, each

57

of you contribute a hymn, some instruction, a revelation, an ecstatic utterance, or the interpretation of such an utterance" (I Corinthians 14.26). Only the women were left out in deference to social convention.

Another letter written by Clement of Rome in A.D. 96, not so very long after Paul, also gives the impression that no one was expected to have observer status only at the Liturgy. The bishop, presbyters, deacons and the rest of the people all have their particular contribution to make. "Let each of you, brethren, make eucharist to God according to his own order, keeping a good conscience and adhering to the appointed rule of his service with all reverence." In other words: "All of you have a job to do, stick to your own and do it well."

This same division of labour which gave everyone a part to play was still practised in the second century. Justin Martyr's descriptions of services in Rome round about A.D. 140 tell us more about what the jobs actually were. It was the bishop's responsibility to preside, preach the sermon and offer the great prayer of thanksgiving. It is made quite clear however that he did not offer all the other prayers or read the lessons. The deacons may have had responsibilities here. Where security mattered there was a certain amount of guard duty to be done. They were certainly given the task of sharing out the bread and wine amongst the congregation, as well as taking them to any who were absent. The rest of the people were expected to 'cry aloud' 'Amen!' and heartily endorse any prayers that were said. They greeted each other with the kiss of peace, brought the gifts of bread and wine for the offering, and received them, now consecrated, at the communion. It is more than likely that there were also hymns or psalms to sing, dialogues to take a part in and other responses to make. When you went to worship you were kept fairly busy. Services could be long but you were not left with time on your hands.

All in all what glimpses we get of the worship of the pre-Nicene church reflect a very real sense of community. It was too spontaneous to be thought of as a logical outcome of the church's response to the events concerning Jesus. Nevertheless it was those events which gave rise to talk about reconciliation, fellowship and life together, and the counterpart of that talk was a growing number of active communities which shared a great deal in common including their joint responsibility for the Liturgy. Of course, from the start, they had to come to terms with the realities of community life. Leaders were required and a measure of organisation. There had to be some rules if things were to run smoothly. Not all were equally gifted and some were more suited to a particular job than others. Distinctions were made, but within the context of an over-riding mutuality. If they were not the same, they were members of a single body. All were equally necessary to the life of the whole so that when it came to the Liturgy, for example, it could no more be celebrated without the people to play their part than it could without an elder or bishop to preside.

If we glance away from this early period and look at the church and its worship at the end of the Middle Ages, prior to the Reformation, we find that the position has changed out of all recognition. The bread and wine are still in evidence but the people rarely receive them. It seems more important that they should be consecrated and the sacrifice of Christ re-presented than that they should be shared in anything like a common meal. The laity have ceased to communicate and by the thirteenth century were only required to do so a minimum of once a year.

In many cases the position was worse. The people not only ceased to communicate, they ceased to attend many of the services. These usually took the form of Low Mass, a less elaborate version of the Liturgy. It dispensed with the choir and could be carried out by a single priest and his assistant, whereas normally a larger clerical staff was required. These simplified arrangements were originally designed to meet the difficulty of catering for increasing numbers of people. They could not all get in to one service, and in order to provide more, resources could no longer be concentrated in one central place. But later on, Low Mass came to be used by the priest as a private and daily devotional exercise. In addition, there was the growing custom of saying Mass like saying prayers, in order to obtain a particular request. The more often it was said, the more likely was the request to be granted, whether it was for a safe journey in this world or a safe passage to the next. Rather than do all this themselves the laity paid the clergy to do it for them. Their offering was not now an integral part of the service. It was given beforehand in order that the service should be held. Where the people were absent, or when present fell to being passive spectators, their parts of the Liturgy, such as communion and offering, tended to be omitted or, in the case of a number of prayers, taken over by the clergy. The deacon who had once led the people's contributions to worship now changed sides and assisted the priest who performed what was left of the Liturgy on his own. Once Latin ceased to be spoken generally but was retained as the language of the Mass, the silent populace could not even understand what was being said. Altogether, an orchestrated piece had become a solo performance.

This enormous change could hardly be described as deliberate and it was generations before the results were seen in perspective. Those involved were no doubt unaware of what was happening to them, just as at the time we are not always aware of what is happening to us.

We have already hinted at some of the reasons. Congregational participation was not so easy to arrange for large public gatherings as for more private domestic occasions. The long basilicas did not help. It was difficult to see and hear properly from the back. It was easy to feel left out though many, it is true, preferred it due to their increasing fear of the elements. It was safer not to be involved. Added to this were problems of discipline which none of us escapes. It was one thing to encourage everyone to join in when the church was a closely knit and highly committed group. It was quite another when many were only nominally Christian and were joining in rather too easily. In unruly times it was not surprising that some emphasis was put on the need to be good enough to take communion however far that was from the outlook of One who tended to ignore the lack of such qualifications and preferred so-called sinners to the self-styled righteous.

If exclusion on moral grounds can be criticised, the Liturgy had nevertheless always been exclusive. Admission was limited and the idea died hard. In the early days the few had been the fully paid up members of a minority movement. It was the Liturgy of the baptised. Once the majority were baptised the old principle of selection kept almost nobody out. Another dividing line now assumes much greater importance. It is not between the church and the world, for such a line becomes difficult to draw. It is between the church members and the clergy. What marks off the few is not baptism but ordination and it is in relation to this that the changes in the Liturgy make most sense.

We can, so to speak, smell the word 'lay' going bad over a long period of time. In the early centuries it meant what it said. The laity were the laos, the people of God. It was a name for the whole church. The minister was a layman just as much as any other member of the community. There may have been some division of labour. There were bishops, elders and deacons, but there was no closed shop. All shared fully in the church's life including the Liturgy.

Perhaps it was unrealistic to expect the old community spirit to continue when larger numbers began to join the church, but certainly if a priesthood of all believers shared by all the people had once been a fact that was soon no longer the case. Priesthood came to be in a class by itself. The majority of church members played an increasingly subordinate role. The term 'lay' was restricted to the non-ordained and took on overtones which are still reflected in our common speech. The layman is an amateur in contrast to the professional. He does not quite make the grade. From the third century on his status in the church progressively declines.

It is not our purpose to trace the history of that decline down to the mediaeval period; in any case much of it is lost in the obscurity of the Dark Ages. However, by the eleventh, twelfth and thirteenth centuries laymen in the bad sense had been robbed of many tasks including administrative ones, and any initiative on their part was regarded as an interference rather than a contribution. They were expected to be quietly submissive. It was not only because the layman was inferior and usually illiterate compared with the educated upper ranks of the clergy. It was not only that there was this fundamental division in mediaeval life between two utterly different groups. There was in addition the clear implication that the laity did not quite make it as the people of God. They were not the genuine article. The church was now virtually equivalent to the clerical orders.

Two features of the Liturgy typify this corruption of the word laity from a synonym for the church to a label for amateur outsiders. One is longstanding. As early as the third century stone and marble walls began to divide the nave from the sanctuary. They became the ultimate symbol of exclusion and can still be seen in some church buildings today. A forbidding screen separates off the altar and choir stalls. Inside this restricted area priests and trained choirs of monks celebrated the Liturgy. The Laity were not admitted. No longer part of the real church they were excluded from the real action and left to watch as best they could.

The second feature was that of increasing elaboration. The Liturgy, especially in the form of High Mass, had grown so complicated that only the practised professional was able to cope. The laity could only feel like amateurs at the game.

Left on the sidelines with nothing to do, something was needed to occupy the time. Books were provided, known as lay-folk's mass books. They were not translations of the Latin Mass, though a few prayers were included. They contained devotional material and, for the illiterate, suitable and often splendid illustrations. In addition to the books various features of the service were deliberately associated with aspects of the Passion of Christ. The laity were to follow the peep-show as best they could in the hope that parts of the Liturgy would trigger off appropriate lines of thought. All these measures were calculated to produce suitable states of mind and heart, and people who thought about what they were barred from doing.

This represents yet another shift of emphasis. The Liturgy was no longer corporate, not only because it was no longer an activity of the whole church, but in another sense as well. The laity may still have been all together although they had ceased to join in, but they were carrying out quite private pursuits. They were not there for the sake of the common life of the Christian community. They had forgotten what Paul emphasised so strongly to the Corinthians, that the aim of worship is to build up the church. They did not, many as they were, become one as they shared the one loaf. It was not the church that was remade at the Eucharist but a collection of single people. Going to church was now a more individualistic affair and what happened had more to do with a man alone and his God than with men together united in Christ.

There is then a tremendous contrast between the Liturgy of the primitive church and that of the Middle Ages. In one case, all joined in, and in the other the majority were left out. If persistence were the deciding factor then the clerically dominated worship which persisted for so long would win hands down, but the reasons for it hardly convince us that the result was a more appropriate expression of the genius of Christianity than the corporate activity it replaced. We may understand but cannot justify a form of worship where the people or laity were forbidden to interrupt instead of being expected to join in. The whole development looks more like a mistake than an achievement.

The Reformers of the sixteenth century apparently agreed, though any improvement in the status of the laity should not be attributed too hastily to their enlightenment alone. For instance, the great disparity between clerical learning and lay ignorance began to break down after the thirteenth century as opportunities for education began to grow. Maybe it became more difficult to keep the laity quite so firmly in their place.

However, the Reformers, led by Luther, Zwingli and Calvin, showed signs of appreciating that the church comprised people, and this was reflected in their attitude to the Liturgy. In a number of ways what went on in worship was made more accessible to the congregation and the congregation was invited to take part in worship. Not all the changes were inspired by a single motive. When the Mass was translated from Latin into the language of the people, for example, it certainly enabled them to share in worship to an extent unknown before, but it was also the logical outcome of the Reformers' stress on the importance of the Word and preaching, and of the need for the people to understand what the Bible had to say to them. Again, if they were to be true to another Reformation emphasis and encourage people to grasp the Christian faith for themselves rather than accept it without thinking, then it had to be made intelligible. The use of the vernacular was therefore much more than a move towards corporate worship, though it contributed much in that direction.

Three other changes may be noted. Some of the prayers which had slipped into the singular when taken over by the professionals were put back into the plural and once again were said by all. The music of trained choirs was exchanged for congregational hymn singing, and Luther led the way as a hymn writer with his 'German psalms for German people'. Of special significance was the fresh insistence that the Mass was neither a spectacle to be watched nor a private pursuit carried out by the priest alone. It was a common action in which all must share. The people's part in the Liturgy was seen to be essential. Just as it was no good preaching to an empty church, so it was useless to break bread with no one there to share it. The Reformers insisted on the communion of the people. This change of heart, not to say revolution, was nicely illustrated at the cathedral in Zurich. In other places the holy table was moved nearer to the people, but in Zurich it was left more or less where it was, in the remote and forbidden area beyond the screen. The people moved instead, and the Lord's Supper found them sitting in the choir stalls round the table, reinstated in the place which had so clearly symbolised their exclusion. They had returned from exile in the nave to reclaim their place again as active participants in worship.

It was not all gain however. Zwingli, who led the invasion of this derestricted zone, also reduced the frequency of celebrating the Lord's Supper to four times a year. Others, like Calvin, who saw more clearly that it is the normal and central act of Christian worship, were not very successful at persuading the people to communicate, and most of them continued to leave after the sermon.

Along with the rest of us, the Reformers were children of their time, and it has often been pointed out that they were more like than unlike their predecessors. They inherited without realising it much of the individualism and clericalism of the mediaeval church. Continuing clergy domination can be illustrated by referring again

63

to the Reformation emphasis on the Word. This had to be preached and its meaning explained. The minister cast himself very much in the role of a teacher and even put on an academic gown to emphasise the point. Worship services became excellent opportunities for instruction, but instruction was carried almost to excess. The concern for the Word resulted in an almost incredible wordiness, and it was the minister who did most of the talking. He not only read the Bible and preached the sermon, but took the opportunity at other points in the service to explain what it was all about. The end result was another form of clericalism. If the laity had been invited back into the restricted zone they were reluctant to accept the invitation as far as communicating was concerned. They preferred the first part of the service to the second, the Word to the Sacrament, but here they were subjected to a monologue where for much of the time the only voice which was raised was that of the preacher.

Clerical domination of worship still persists. If Roman Catholics are familiar with the Mass at which the priest performs the objective sacrifice whilst the rest look on, members of the Free Churches are equally familiar with services at which the minister says all the prayers, including the 'Amen', preaches the sermon, reads the lessons and even makes the announcements. There are no service books and there is nothing for the congregation to say together apart from the Lord's Prayer. The only other point at which all join in is when it comes to the hymns which, admittedly, are a fairly prominent feature of some traditions. This relatively passive role of the congregation is so familiar that it has become the norm. Any departure from it is initially regarded with some misgivings.

The Reformers certainly contributed to the restoration of the people's rights in the Liturgy, but perhaps we owe even more to what is generally referred to as the Liturgical Movement. A detailed account of it could easily degenerate into a catalogue of names and dates. The fact that there are so many is in itself something to be thankful for and indicates how prolific this movement has been. We must be content however to make three general points.

First, the origins of the movement, in both its early and later stages, are probably to be found in the Roman Catholic Church, and in particular within the Benedictine Order in the early nineteenth and then again in the early twentieth century. But it also looks like one of those movements, not unknown in history, which appear to spring up simultaneously in a number of places. It is certainly true to say that it became increasingly widespread in all branches of the church.

Second, the movement refers to a general revival of interest in the Liturgy. Early and later stages were mentioned. The early stage had a rather backward look. It shared in the Romantic Movement's love of the past. Guéranger, the monk who started it all, wanted to revive the ancient traditions of the church and relied very heavily on the thought and practice of the Middle Ages. One of his greatest achievements was the restoration of the Gregorian chant, named after Gregory, the Pope we have met before in connection with the Gregorian Sacramentary, who was also an ardent supporter of the Benedictine Order.

It would be foolish to dismiss what almost became an obsession with the past, especially where it leads to the rediscovery of riches that are ours for the inheriting. We must be wary however of falling into merely antiquarian pursuits which admire ancient traditions for their own sake. Nothing is good simply because it is old.

Third, the later stages of the movement have shown a much greater concern for the needs of the contemporary church. Digging up the past has given way to caring for the present: archaeology to pastoralia. There has been growing agreement on a number of recurring themes, including the centrality of the service we have called the Liturgy, embracing both Word and Sacrament; the need for the Liturgy to have a shape and be properly ordered; and the integral relationship between worship and the mission of the church. One of the most persistent convictions however has been that when we come to do the Liturgy we must all join in; and it is only fair to add that but for the insights of the Liturgical Movement we should not be advocating congregational participation so confidently as we are advocating it now.

If asked why the congregation should be actively involved in worship this brief historical survey has already touched on most of the arguments advanced. We have seen how it corresponds to the life style of the earliest communities which sprang up as a spontaneous response to the original events concerning Jesus of Nazareth. If the Christian tradition moved in a different direction for more than a thousand years, there has been a surprising turnabout since the Reformation and more particularly during the twentieth century. There is growing unanimity that in this particular instance it was a mistake to depart from the practice of the apostolic church.

We have also referred to a quite crucial insight regained in comparatively recent times. The church is the people of God, not the clerical few, and anything which belongs to the church from mission

65

to worship belongs to all the people. When the church comes to do the Liturgy, its most distinctive corporate activity, it is quite untrue to our understanding of the church if to all intents and purposes only the ordained members of the laity do it, whilst the rest of the baptised are demoted to the role of bystanders.

We hinted at another consideration when referring to the mediaeval congregation, totally excluded from the main action of the Mass, busy with its own private thoughts as it meditated in the nave. This could foster a lack of corporateness in a different sense, and that is the idea that I go to worship not so much to do something as a member of the community but to foster my own private relationship to God. I go to make my communion not to be re-made as part of a community. It reflects an understanding of Christianity largely derived from the western intellectual tradition. In the end it believes that the reality with which God deals is a collection of self-contained individuals rather than the whole family of mankind in which individuals are inextricably bound up with each other and cannot fulfil even their individuality alone.

Corporate worship does not guarantee a more balanced point of view, but it can encourage a greater sense of belonging to each other and the recognition that life, above all the reconciled life, is a social and not a purely private affair. Literally to perform the words and actions of the Liturgy in concert suggests that we live in concert and that in the end it is in concert that we are brought to our full and glorious potential.

Added to these arguments are more practical considerations. Where people are involved they are more likely to be interested. It is easier to attend to what you are doing than to what someone else is doing. Again, although worship is not primarily an opportunity for instruction as some of the Reformers seemed to think, one of its incidental benefits is to teach many things, and people are likely to learn more as participants than as passive receivers. 'All-join-in' is not only a sound liturgical principle, it is a sound educational one as well.

Those then are some lines of argument in favour of the congregation joining in. They are not foolproof. It is no doubt possible to argue the other way. We must be alive to the possibility that we are imposing our own modern, democratic outlook on worship rather than discovering anything like a Christian norm. Even that would not matter of course so long as we recognise the recommendation for what it is, namely something for us and for our time if not for everyone all the time. Nevertheless our decision to advocate the full participation of everyone in the Liturgy is not entirely unreasonable to common sense, nor out of step with the Bible, nor with what has been learned from the long experience of the church. It is in accord with many contemporary voices. Indeed, as with so many aspects of the church's life today, we are not lacking in suggestions which commend a wide measure of agreement about what ought to be done. What is needed is greater persistence and a more dogged determination to carry them out.

What then are some of the practical implications of a determination to turn the Liturgy into an occasion when all join in?

One useful rule of thumb is to leave as little as possible to the minister. No longer is he to be a liturgical Pooh-Bah. Obviously something must be left to him if we are to continue to ordain people to the ministry, and even in the most anti-clerical circles someone looking remarkably like a minister usually emerges. But if he is not to do everything, what is he to do? There are at least two types of answer. They are not mutually exclusive and we had better state them both.

The first suggests that certain specific tasks are reserved to him alone. He can do them and other people cannot. They are however far fewer in number than anyone might guess after observing a good deal of Christian worship. In the pre-Nicene church there were only two. One was the sermon and the other the great prayer of thanksgiving. It is worth noting that the minister was not referred to as the celebrant but the president. He did not celebrate the Liturgy. He had two specific parts to play. For the rest he presided over something which was celebrated by all the people.

This is not the place to embark on a lengthy discussion of the doctrine of the ministry. There are however several good and practical reasons for giving a man special responsibility for Word and Sacrament focused in the sermon and the eucharistic prayer. If the church is to be any use at all to others it must be properly nourished itself. In order to minister it must receive a ministry. It must listen to the Gospel and feed on the body and blood of Christ. If it is to tell the Story it must also hear the Story. It is the minister's job to see that this is so. But the nourishment must be of the right kind. The church must not be misled. It must be kept true to the best apostolic traditions. The teachings and actions by which the church has always lived must be injected into this part of the body living now. This can be ensured by carefully handing on those traditions from one generation of trained ministers to the next and by charging them to build up the church accordingly and keep it in good order. Better still the congregation can be saved from going seriously wrong by being kept in touch with the wider church. They need to pay attention to other Christians and not close up into idiosyncratic groups. It is in isolation that Christians are most likely to fall out of the orbit of anything remotely recognisable as the holy, catholic and apostolic church. The minister can be a convenient link man between the great church and the smaller local group, representing the one to the other. The idea is a very ancient one. It goes back to the time when in theory only one Eucharist was celebrated by the bishop in each place. If more than one service had to be held, in outlying districts as well as in the town centre, these were thought of as extensions of the bishop's Eucharist. The ministers were regarded as his assistants and representatives rather than as independent agents acting on their own.

Focused then in this one person and his special responsibility for Word and Sacrament is the church's concern for what it must receive if it is to give anything to the world, together with its concern for the good ordering of its life, the maintenance of its finest traditions and the unity of its many parts with the whole. Few may wish to quarrel with such sensible arrangements.

Questions do remain however. Could not the minister still be responsible for all these things without reserving to himself the liturgical sermon and the prayer of thanksgiving? He can see that the Story is faithfully told without actually telling it himself. He can see that adequate sermons are preached without always being the preacher. He can make sure that the Sacraments are 'duly administered' without actually administering them. The prayer of thanksgiving could be said by one of the congregation properly instructed and at the invitation of the rest. Better still the congregation could say it together. If it is important to get the words right then the approved formula can be written down as in many cases it already is. The traditions of the church can be preserved in print, and most of us can now read—a simple fact which is often overlooked.

But the most serious hesitations arise when different arrangements are made for the prayer of thanksgiving from those for the sermon. If both are reserved to the minister of Word and Sacrament that at least is consistent, but in most churches today lay people, 'preachers' and 'readers' are a familiar sight in the pulpit, and if anything is reserved to the minister it is the prayer of thanksgiving, or more strictly, the consecration of the elements. Both Word and Sacrament

68

should be handled with care and respect, but if this can be satisfactorily arranged in the case of the Word so that a layman is allowed to preach, cannot similar arrangements be made with regard to the Sacrament for which, incidentally, a good deal less is required in terms of gifts and training?

Where the consecration is singled out from every other part of the Liturgy for special treatment, does it imply a sacerdotal view which belongs to mediaeval times rather than to either the early church or today? Is it a view we still wish to defend? Arguments about good order, handing on the apostolic tradition, nourishing the church and maintaining its unity may add up to something of a case for an ordained ministry, but they begin to sound like rationalisations when used to justify the reservation of the act of consecration to one particular man. The same suspicion falls on those who point out that what is done by one man is done in a representative capacity on behalf of all. Such a representative is hardly necessary when all could act together.

However, our main point is not to argue a case but to mention a point of view and to underline that even here what the minister must do in the Liturgy because no one else is authorised to do it, is very minimal indeed.

The second answer to the question about the distinctive role of the minister is not that he has a number of specific tasks or even a single one reserved to himself, but that he has a special role to play in relation to all tasks which belong to the whole church. His distinctiveness is defined in terms of form rather than content. He is to be a minister and to take the form of a servant in all things, or, as current jargon would have it, he is to be an 'enabler'. He is not to do jobs instead of the church, or to do a job which the rest of the church is not called to do. He enables the church to do its job.

Two familiar images nicely illustrate the role of the minister as enabler and a more adequate understanding of the laity. The church is wrongly thought of as fielding a clerical team to play the game whilst the vast majority form a supporters club to pay the fees and cheer them on. It is better to turn the picture on its head. All members of the church are in the team and go out onto the field. If any stay behind to support it is the clergy, but better still they are to be thought of as trainers and managers who enable the team to play. Or again, the church, especially when it meets to do the Liturgy, is wrongly thought of as a small group of actors who perform the drama and tell the Story whilst the vast majority sit in the audience and watch. It is more adequate to regard all the members as actors. Everyone is on stage. If anyone is left out it is the minister, not to sit and watch but to produce and stage manage the play, and enable the company to perform.

In terms of the bare bones of the Liturgy (see page 4) it is the church that reads the Bible and proclaims the Gospel in preaching. It is the church which says its prayers, makes its offering, gives thanks and shares a loaf and a cup of wine. It is the church which sings its praise in psalms and songs. It is the church which plays the game of celebration and tells the Story, and it is the minister who enables the church to do so.

His enabling or servicing will take various forms. At the heart of the matter he will see to it that the people's attention is constantly drawn to the One they confess as Lord. He will share with the church relevant information about the Bible and the Christian tradition which only he may have had the time to acquire. He is a key resource person though he is not necessarily and by definition the expert theologian. He may train the people in certain necessary skills and seek out and develop useful aptitudes. Initially he may need to drill them in common action and choral speaking and, refusing to be satisfied with a poor performance, rehearse them until they get it right. He will teach the newcomers how to join in, indeed imaginative training sessions on doing an adequate Liturgy may be the best form of preparation for church membership. Here the community comes to self expression. This may be the only distinctive thing the newly baptised will need to do with other Christians. To take part with understanding is to know what it means to belong to those who are committed to tell the Story.

The minister will also have to make practical arrangements, rehearse the proceedings and co-ordinate diverse activities. He will contribute much by a wise understanding of human nature and some insight into the dynamics of groups. As we shall see he may need to be an expert discussion leader and a skilful drafter of material. At whatever point progress is blocked and the people are prevented from fulfilling their liturgy, it is his responsibility to open up the way. If he cannot do so himself then he enables by finding someone who can.

If the minister has additional gifts, such as that of 'stirring speech' or prophetic insight, so much the better, though other people, given the opportunity and encouragement might reveal that they have them as well. If by virtue of his gifts the minister is given certain tasks in the Liturgy itself, it is wise to remember that it is for the sake of those gifts rather than by virtue of any rights bestowed on him at his ordination. If what has been described is thought to be too mundane a task for such a lofty calling, requiring a nation of shopkeepers rather than a spiritual élite, such notions may reveal a residual clericalism. If lofty callings and spiritual élitism have a place, they, like everything else, are possibilities for all the people of God and are not the prerogative of any single member of the body of Christ.

Should the minister preside? Perhaps so, but in the manner in which an unobtrusive leader can make all the difference to the life of a community, or the manner in which a conductor presides over an orchestra. An invitation to conduct (a service) should not be an invitation to come and do a solo performance but to elicit music from all the players.

The minister therefore may preside, represent, keep things in good order, link the local church with the great church, care for apostolic tradition, see to it that the church is properly nourished; but in worship as in mission, as little as possible will be left to him when it comes to the actual task. Although he may do any number of things, as one layman amongst others, he does nothing as minister. He is ordained to enable the people to do it all.

Another rule of thumb follows naturally enough from the first though, as we shall see, it is still not sufficient. First, leave as little as possible to the minister. Second, do as much as you can together. This is not to decry the division of labour, but it is to make sure that at every point opportunities for participation are open to all.

Looking back again over the bare bones of the Liturgy, the opening words in which the people greet one another and their Lord, remind themselves of what they are about, and have their attention called to the object of worship, can take the form of a dialogue between the president and the people, like this fairly traditional one (words in italics are said by the president):

*I welcome you in the name of the Father and of the Son
and of the Holy Spirit*
and we welcome one another
we are here as members of the one human family
we are here because we can say together: Jesus is Lord
we have come to tell his Story
and be re-made as a community
we have come to worship our God
and to identify ourselves with his ways

71

'To whom could you liken me
and who could be my equal?' says the Holy One
Yahweh is an everlasting God
he created the boundaries of the earth
He does not grow tired or weary
his understanding is beyond fathoming
He gives strength to the wearied
he strengthens the powerless
To whom could you liken God?
What image could you contrive of him?
It is the God who said 'Let light shine out of darkness'
who has shone in our hearts
to give the light of the knowledge of the glory of God
in the face of Christ

Everyone is involved from the beginning. It need not be between president and people but between sections of the congregation. In a more informal setting it would include the friendly exchanges and enquiries that most people indulge in when they meet. The minister does not need to make a grand entry into the room immediately before the service commences, as if to imply that the one person really needed to begin is now here. He will be there sitting with and greeting the rest, and will simply take the chair when all are ready. His initiative is like the conductor's. It is not the start of a solo. It enables everyone to begin.

Moving on, there are many ways of saying our prayers together. We can be free to use them all or to find those which best suit a particular community. Written prayers can be read. What we might call 'the classics' which bear repeating on many occasions can be memorised. Individuals can contribute brief prayers of their own. Suggestions, often called biddings, can be made about subjects for intercession, either vocally at the time or in writing beforehand. The announcements, especially if they include information about the local community as well as the activities of the congregation, are appropriate at this point. Local people from inside and outside the church can be allowed a few disciplined minutes to describe their work or some issue that matters to them. Items from the local and national papers can be referred to and the relevant cuttings posted on display boards in the room. In these and other ways the people's attention is drawn to areas of concern.

Silence is then kept during which no one is forced to listen to someone else's prayers but has time to pray in his own way. These individual prayers can then be gathered together in a very brief summary like the collect we mentioned earlier, or in an exchange between the president and the people like this familiar one:

Lord hear our prayer
And let our cry come unto thee

or this more satisfactory one:

Father this is our prayer
Help us to know and to do your will

These exchanges (sometimes referred to as versicles and responses) can also be the signal for the next set of biddings or suggestions to be made. One form of prayer which should not normally be allowed in the Liturgy is a lengthy prayer said by any one individual whether he is presiding or not. It does not hold the attention and more often than not it is an insensitive imposition of one man's devotions on all the rest. Finally, the people's 'Amen' should not degenerate into the minister's way of saying: 'I've finished!'

If reading the Bible is not the prerogative of the minister, neither need it be restricted to the lay reader usually seen at the lectern. The regular practice of one person reading to everyone else is probably based on the once correct but now ill-founded assumption that no one else can read. That does not mean we should never have the benefit of listening to someone read well but it ought to be reserved for the passages which lend themselves to that kind of treatment. Otherwise there are other possibilities which involve more people. Some passages can be broken up into parts for several voices or sections of the congregation. Reading round in turn a verse or sentence at a time need not be so disastrous as it sounds. All can read aloud together or in a period of quiet read the passage to themselves, always assuming that everyone has a copy of the same version of the Bible!

Any gifts of money can be collected from the people as they arrive or at some other convenient moment. The offering, the first of the four actions, is brought to the table by the people. In the early days of the church it was their special liturgy par excellence. Originally made up of gifts in kind out of which the bread and wine were taken for the Lord's Supper it is now usually made up of money together with the one loaf and the common cup. On certain occasions other representative gifts may be included, but at the very least all will stand together at this moment when the church gives itself again to the Christ of whom it speaks.

That all will communicate goes without saying. The method of sharing the bread and wine should be watched. Sometimes called 'the administration' it can easily become clericalised. Where help is needed, it should be given by specially appointed deacons; better still, congregations can develop simple manners or customs whereby the loaf and cup are passed from one to the other, each being served by his neighbour.

Psalms and hymns and songs are usually corporate affairs and need not delay us. Where there is a choir, care should be taken that it leads the community singing from behind rather than performs too many expert pieces from the front.

A word should be said about the kiss of peace or Pax mentioned in the New Testament at the end of several letters and in a number of early descriptions of worship. In the primitive church it appeared in the Liturgy before the offering though it was later moved elsewhere. In some respects it was the greeting which began the second part of the Liturgy after the catechumens had been dismissed and only the baptised remained. The faithful now greeted each other with a holy kiss, but it was not to become a mere formality. Matthew 5.23f. was very much to the point:

> "If, when you are bringing your gift to the altar, you suddenly remember that your brother has a grievance against you, leave your gift where it is before the altar. First go and make your peace with your brother, and only then come back and offer your gift." (N.E.B.)

Any differences were to be reconciled and good relationships established before people came to the Eucharist. Here was a corporate action which focused the life together which is so characteristic of the faith and is a fundamental reason why we should all join in.

The straightforward kiss has been modified. It can be replaced by an embrace, a bow, a handshake, by joining hands in a circle in the manner of 'Auld Lang Syne', and with traditional exchanges such as

> *The peace of the Lord be always with you*
> and with thy spirit

or their contemporary counterpart.

A little imagination could turn the Pax into a more realistic

74

opportunity for people to exchange reconciling words and gestures, and to show their friendship and their interest in each other. For example, it should be possible, and often very convenient, to have a break in the service, when drinks could be served and an opportunity given for people to talk. Conversation might be more appropriate at this point than after the dismissal at the end when the people, sent away, should disperse and hurry back into the world. On informal occasions, the Pax could be extended even more. After the readings and sermon and before the relatively concise actions of the Eucharist, the kiss of peace could be replaced by a meal not unlike the earlier love feasts and fellowship meals of the primitive church.

The sermon, at first sight, presents few opportunities for participation, and as we have seen, it has at times been reserved as a prerogative of the ordained minister. Another point of view would see no reason why this should be so and every reason why others should be involved, although where there are gifted preachers it would be foolish not to make the most of them.

In making the sermon a more corporate activity, care should be taken that the element of telling the Story, of announcing the good news and of proclamation, is not entirely lost (see page 18). This can happen, for example, when the sermon is replaced by group discussion about the Bible passages for the week, or an aspect of faith and experience, or some contemporary issue. Time and circumstances may permit a preliminary exchange of views which may be interesting and valuable but it is usually inconclusive, not in the sense of leaving questions unanswered, that must always be so, but in the sense that what good news the church feels it has and can announce, however tentatively, is left unstated and unproclaimed. Nothing has been made very clear and often the real discipline of sharpening up what can be said has been avoided. The same can be true of so-called dialogue sermons. Open-ended conversations between two people may be excellent preparation for preaching and they can be done in public to great effect, but they are not the same as the proclamation that is made in the Liturgy. There is a finality about the liturgical sermon. It promulgates the outcome of our exploration, however interim that may be; it is not the exploration itself.

Group discussion, in relation to preaching, is better done beforehand as part of the preparation for what will be proclaimed much more concisely in the sermon at the Liturgy. Groups can be used in the Liturgy, but they should not be expected to achieve the impossible. They are not able to preach, though they are well able to share concerns with each other or even discuss a particular problem at length. Here is a corporate way of interceding which could sometimes replace more traditional ways of praying.

Provided we safeguard this element of proclamation the sermon could be a more corporate affair and there is no reason why it should not be followed by a descent from the pulpit to a seat amongst the people for questions and conversation, reactions and comments. The sermon can also be enriched by what others are prepared to say about Jesus and his Story.

In these and other ways solo performances can be avoided, and all sections of the orchestra can be brought into play in the conduct of the Liturgy. Everyone will require copies of the score. Hymn books, bibles and prayer books will be needed; but better still, a loose-leaf worship book into which all kinds of material, songs, prayers, readings, dialogues, affirmations of faith, and orders of worship can be inserted, and also thrown away when they cease to be of use.

Seating arrangements can make a big difference. Rows and rows of pews in basilican fashion, suggesting the audience–actor relationship, will not help. Where possible people should sit together round the table. Traditional buildings can be adapted along these lines. Large floor spaces need not be despised. They can be divided into separate and more intimate areas for different activities including an area for the kind of informal conversation and social intercourse mentioned in relation to the Pax. Where large numbers make it difficult for everyone to sit round the table in any meaningful sense, it may be possible to sit in separate circles round a central table. Each circle could represent the membership of an active cell in the church's life, a house group or task force which in practice experiences life together outside of the Liturgy. Although it has been allowed to hinder participation in the past, size should not be thought of as necessarily excluding corporate activity. Different things are possible on different occasions and many of the suggestions we have made are possible on all occasions.

So far so good. First leave as little as possible to the minister and then do as much as you can together. But does this go far enough? We are left with the impression that all join in but only to a limited extent. The minister decides what is going to be done and then allows, or maybe cajoles, the congregation into carrying out his pre-arranged plan. They act out pre-determined roles. He may enable them to do the Liturgy, but the Liturgy they are invited to do appears to be his and not theirs.

Of course, to a certain extent, the minister is also under orders. A significant element, including the basic pattern and the lectionary, are as fixed for him as for anyone else. But in the large area of freedom and variety which remains he is still operating as a benign dictator, telling other people what to do. What is required is not only corporate action when the Liturgy actually takes place, but corporate responsibility when the Liturgy is prepared. What form it takes will be varied to suit the people concerned. In the case of a small group, all of them may well be involved in planning every Liturgy they celebrate. In larger congregations representative individuals or existing groups may take it in turns to form a worship workshop. We should prevent it from becoming the concern of a few; one sectional interest amongst many in the church's life. We do not want a clerical group to replace a clergyman. Opportunities and responsibilities should be shared by all.

If all join in at the planning stage, it may help to avoid the mistake of forcing people into over-restrictive liturgical moulds which demand certain skills and exclude others. Instead the Liturgy can be adapted to make full use of the skills which people already have. Not everyone is good at public speaking, reading aloud, saying prayers or playing the organ. Those who are not may be gifted at writing, listening, painting, dancing, or playing any one of a whole range of instruments, to mention only a few of the many possibilities. If the performers are there from the beginning their abilities can be discovered before it is too late. Once we are rid of our prejudices, it is surprising how many gifted people can be employed, so that the act of worship which results is in a very real sense their own.

This corporate responsibility should certainly extend to preaching. It is probably a mistake to allow group discussion to replace the sermon in the Liturgy, but it is equally mistaken not to use some form of group discussion to prepare the sermon for the Liturgy. We shall return to the point again when we talk about relevance under the heading 'Down-to-earth'. A single illustration must suffice. Liturgical preaching, as distinct from many other valuable forms of address on other occasions, is concerned to tell the Story and proclaim the good news associated with Jesus of Nazareth. The minister, because of his training, may put in some preliminary work on the three scriptural passages indicated by the lectionary (see page 18) for that week. They are of unique importance to the church because they stand so close to the events which interest her and provide the nearest to first-hand information we can get. The minister brings the results of his preliminary investigations to the group so that in answering their questions initial difficulties can be overcome and completely mistaken interpretations avoided. In this way the group is enabled to discuss with understanding and can go on to explore what the passages have to say when seen from their contemporary vantage points. The group should try to reach a common mind, though it may have to settle for an untidy though enriching difference of opinion.

If the sermon is to take the form of straightforward speech, then a member of the group, gifted in organising material and speaking in public, will go away and prepare what he is going to say in the light of the discussion and proclaim it at the Liturgy. The minister may be considered for the job, but it should not be presumed that he is the only likely candidate. If the sermon is going to take a less conventional form, then it is still necessary for someone to prepare the substance of the proclamation so that the method of communication arises out of what has to be communicated and is kept in place as a means to an end rather than allowed to become an end in itself.

If such an approach appears to have no room for the 'gifted preacher' three things ought to be said in reply. First, a definite place has been given to him already with the qualification that he should exercise his gift in co-operation with others and not in too individualistic a manner. Second, we should be wary of cultivating the taste for gifted preachers if it still exists. They are often enjoyed for other reasons than that they tell the Story and build up the church. Third, the gifted preacher is probably more like the man with the gift of wise speech mentioned in I Corinthians 12, than the man who delivers the liturgical sermon. He must be given the opportunity to exercise his gift, but he should be regarded as the exception rather than the rule.

The preparation of the sermon is one of the best places for a worship workshop to start. Although it is wrong to build every item in the service round too narrow a theme, a number of details will be suggested by the emerging content of the proclamation. For example, it will suggest some, though not all, of the subjects for the prayers, and those aspects of the Story which have received special attention should certainly be referred to in the thanksgiving for what God has done above all in Christ.

In advocating a greater degree of corporate responsibility for the Liturgy we must be realistic and good stewards of people's time. Without denying the centrality of worship it would be wrong to encourage people to spend a disproportionate amount of time preparing services when they ought to be doing other things, and it would be unrealistic to assume that they will find the time or sustain their interest if stretched too far.

If the Liturgy is to be a corporate enterprise in this thorough-going sense, then a measure of simplicity will be required in at least two respects, and it might well be advocated on other grounds as well. First, there is a world of difference between the attempt to have something novel each week, often degenerating into a frantic and wearisome search for new ideas, and on the other hand making sure that a fairly settled pattern is done well. The settled pattern is much to be preferred. It does not mean that the Liturgy should be closed to the enrichment of new ideas, new gifts and fresh approaches. Nor does it exclude the possibility that on great festal occasions the church will go to town. Again, just because the Liturgy is regarded as *the* service there is no suggestion that a variety of other services cannot flourish alongside it (see page 3). But there should be a familiar sameness about this one. It is the staple diet: 'bread-and-butter' worship. People should not be asked to engage in a continuous quest for something new but to work within an agreed formula which is always open to criticism and adjustment but has proved from patient evolution to be of enduring value to that particular Christian community.

Second, there will be a measure of simplicity, in that the agreed formula will also include simple and regular procedures for getting things done which the community has found to be workable. It is not usually necessary for the same people to come to lengthy meetings about the Liturgy week after week. There may be periodic reviews with more time for thorough-going discussion, but apart from group preparation for preaching a good deal of the work can be shared out in the form of individual responsibilities within an agreed corporate policy. One person can be left to arrange the intercessions for example, seeing to it that the content is carefully prepared, the outside world fully represented, and those taking part properly instructed. The music master will have all the resources of the community at his finger tips and bring them fully into play. Others can see that copies of all written material from songs to prayers are available and appoint various people to bring the offering to the table and provide the bread and wine in turn.

Even sermon preparation need not necessarily add yet another meeting to those which already exist. Some form of discussion and spirituality is usually an ongoing feature of most church organisations. There are sectional meetings, Bible study and house groups, groups engaged in one task or another which all give time to talking about the faith. In addition, there is the daily Bible reading still advocated by some as part of every Christian's private and family discipline. All these activities are usually haphazard and unrelated, but they could be used to reflect on the scriptural passages for the week. This in itself would give a sense of doing something together and would be good preparation for the Liturgy, where the people would not listen for the first time to strange words but words already read and thought about. By meeting groups or their representatives and talking to individuals some of the harvest of all this reflection could be gathered, if not all of it every week, then parts of it in turn, and built into the preparation of the liturgical sermon.

Much of what has been said about the need for simplicity has been illustrated against the background of the more familiar pattern of congregational life. In the case of a smaller group, meeting for example in a house, one can imagine the arrangements being very simple indeed, and the Liturgy being so integrated with the life of the group that the preparations almost go without saying.

In the last resort what is looked for is nothing more elaborate than an attitude of mind. It may not matter overmuch if the minister, for the sake of simplicity and convenience, not to mention his gifts, has a few more jobs than anyone else. What does matter is if he comes to regard worship as his special preserve. "You have your field of expertise. I have mine." Granted the need in practice for some division of labour, the minister's expertise is to enable the church to fulfil the calling that belongs to all its members. Liturgical affairs, like talking and eating food, are everybody's business, and the enabler is uniquely fulfilled when he is declared redundant.

In conclusion, a word should be said about the children. They should be invited to take a full and responsible part in the Liturgy as well. 'All-join-in' does mean 'all', not in the sense of the public in general but in the sense of all the members of the church. This will raise difficulties for people who believe that church membership is only for those who are old enough to decide for themselves. On these grounds the Liturgy of the baptised is not for children, certainly not the younger ones. Such a position is logical enough. The problem is that life is not quite so tidy. If there are two well defined groups, one completely unattached to the church and its worship in any shape or form, the other clearly committed to telling the Christian

Story, there is also a third. It includes adults as well as children. Without being totally committed, they are certainly not unattached. They live further in than the outside edges of the community's life. They could be regarded as the catechumenate. They are on the way to faith. In the case of the children of Christian parents, they are well within the family of the church. Any later decision about baptism and membership will have more to do with staying in or getting out than with entering for the first time. Such children are in a different relationship to the church than those whose parents rarely if ever come. Whatever the theology, in reality they are on the inside and ought therefore to take part in the community's most characteristic activity, even if some aspects of it have to be reserved for those who have come of age and are fully committed. Those who practice infant baptism need not logically make any such reservations. But again life is not so tidy and they often do, in complete contrast to the Orthodox churches for example which have literally spoonfed their children on the sacramental bread and wine.

Practical objections to children participating in the Liturgy sometimes loom larger than theological ones, though the objections often tell us more about our worship than about our offsprings. It is said that they will not understand, with a surprising forgetfulness of how little adults understand. It is then said that they will get bored and will be put off for life if too much is expected of them too soon. Perhaps they are bored for much the same reasons as many adults are bored. Like them, and even more so, they are largely excluded from what is going on and remain inactive observers who are continually told to be quiet and keep still. Busy children are not usually bored children. It is also said that children are a nuisance. Their restless behaviour disturbs the service. Granted that there probably is a threshold below which babies and toddlers are best left in the crèche, a good deal of restlessness will be the direct result of the boredom and inactivity already referred to. Turn the children into responsible participants and they will usually rise to the occasion. Objections to a limited amount of noise and disturbance, a normal feature of most family gatherings, probably arises from an excessively formal approach to worship and the identification of an authentic atmosphere with an unbroken quiet, fragile enough to break at the cry of a single child. Without denying for a moment the need for silence, it is strange how we learn to cope with noise at many points in life, but are often unable to cope with it in worship. We might add that if quiet meditation is an important aspect of

81

Christian experience maybe the Liturgy, with its rather purposeful action, is not the time or place for too much of it.

Finding more room for the children does not mean replacing one rigid rule with another. In many churches it has been wrongly assumed that you should never have them in for more than a curtain raiser to the real thing. There is no need to swing to the opposite extreme and never take them out! For example, it may sometimes make good sense to replace the sermon with an alternative though related activity, though it is better to avoid any talk of lessons and classes. We have overemphasised the value of instruction. Neither preaching nor worship are primarily concerned with teaching, although sharing in the life of the Christian community, focused in the Liturgy, will be a significant educational experience as the child and the man are formed by a living tradition.

Children will be encouraged to join in worship not merely by inserting items especially for their benefit, or by letting them have their turn while indulged parents look on; and certainly not by bringing everything or anything down to a childish level. Their understanding may not be an adult understanding, but they can do what adults are doing. They may not realise the meaning of a dialogue or the full implications of a creed or prayer, but they can read them with the rest if they are written out in bold print and good straightforward prose. They will enjoy finding things in Bibles and song books. Some will read the lessons or play in the band. They can contribute to the intercessions. Collecting up the gifts of the people is not a children's job, but it is a job that children can do. The same is true of serving at communion. Why should not a child take his place amongst those who distribute the bread and wine? Indeed it is interesting to ask what these children, in a real sense part of the family, should not be allowed to do, and the answer might be surprising. Perhaps they should be excluded from taking part in the offering. In the early church it was the special contribution of the baptised. Children may be there, but until they have decided to throw in their lot and self-consciously committed themselves to the Story that is told, they should not carry to the table the loaf and the cup. Actually eating bread and drinking wine could be a different matter. These have much more to do with what is given to us irrespective of our own self-giving, and there may be a case for children sharing in the family meal. If that is unacceptable then the catechumenate might at least be allowed to receive unconsecrated bread.

But details, however intriguing, are less important than the general principle. By their full participation in its preparation and performances, the Liturgy must be seen to belong to all the people of God and not to the clerical few.

Multi-media

What has been suggested so far may sound rather conventional, especially to those who have heard rumours of a more adventurous approach to worship which really carries the hallmark of the twentieth century. Far from recovering older features of the Liturgy this contemporary emphasis appears to be giving it an entirely new look.

For example people have been seen to dance in church. The movements may be choreographed for the expert or better still called out in square-dance style so that even the flat-footed novice can join in. Films replace the sermon. Visual aids illustrate what still remains to be said. Slide projectors bring events to life and provide concrete images for prayer. Photographs and pictures evoke memories of the communion of saints. Mime speaks louder than words. The Story is dramatised rather than told. The whole congregation appears to be caught up in the action of the play. Not content to stand or kneel for prayer and go to the table for communion, they move in processions, carry their banners and placards, physically express their sorrow, fear and joy. People clap when they approve. They are not afraid to touch each other, to hold hands or embrace. Bright clothes are worn and cheerful decorations suggest the time of celebration. Symbols and folk art create a rich environment which cannot all be taken in at a glance. There is more to see than usual. Lighting effects are reminiscent of the theatre. We are on stage with its spots, floods of colour, strobes and blackouts. The candles burn. We smell the incense. We write and draw. Where we are still expected to have ears, we hear taped interviews, pre-recorded messages, sounds from a week-day and stereophonic music ranging from classical through jazz to pop.

Liturgies which offer such a wide range of experiences are sometimes referred to as multi-media worship. Further examples must be looked for elsewhere. It is not our purpose here to present a collection of ideas any more than it is to discourage experiments. Rather we must try, as we have done all along, to provide a firm framework of understanding which alone can supply the freedom to venture into more exotic country without becoming so absorbed with the immediate terrain that we lose our sense of direction.

We are presented then with a second variation on a theme, which the present generation has contributed to the ongoing liturgical life of the church. Its very nickname—'multi-media'—suggests a concern about communication, but we shall characterise it chiefly in two other ways. The first owes a good deal to the influence which culture has on worship. It can be seen as a move away from those purely verbal forms of expression which are so closely associated with an admiration for reason. The second characteristic is more easily justified by theological arguments, which is not to suggest they are its cause. It represents a more positive attitude to the material world which, among other things, has fostered the growth of modern science in our civilisation. Both characteristics reflect something of the strengths and limitations of a Western frame of mind. We shall look at each of them in turn.

To revert briefly to the concern with communication, current dissatisfaction with conventional ways of doing things has more than a single cause. Rational arguments can certainly be put forward for abandoning the old methods and in some instances reasonably objective tests can be applied. Take the twenty to twenty-five minute sermon as an example. In the traditional form of an uninterrupted monologue it has come in for a good deal of well-deserved criticism. A useful test for any preacher to apply is to ask his hearers to give a brief resumé of his material. In many cases what they heard will be somewhat different from what he thought he had said, always assuming they had listened.

The conventional sermon can be an indifferent means of communication, though it should not be banished too hastily into exile. Most people cannot preach effectively, but a minority can. Whilst the majority should not be encouraged to feel that preaching sermons is the be-all and end-all of their ministry, the church should not deprive itself of the special gifts of the few. Where a man can stir his hearers and build up the church with the gift of speech, he should be given every opportunity to do so.

Even a twenty minute monologue might be effective if the audience put more effort into the work of listening, especially when the speaker has little immediate appeal. The speaker himself often fails to observe elementary rules about using direct forms of speech with clear landmarks plotting the line of thought and plenty of concrete narrative and pictorial images, instead of undifferentiated and convoluted prose. Again it is too readily assumed that a sermon, like a lecture, is primarily concerned to impart information and ideas rather than to tell a Story and point to a vision. It may not matter too much if we do not remember, as long as for a moment we saw.

But when all that has been said, and without ruling the traditional sermon entirely out of court, many would agree that there are better methods of communicating and that some of the insights of the adult educationalists are a good deal more to the point than too much blown up talk about the art of preaching. They suggest that more is communicated through modest forms of exchange and dialogue than through grandiose proclamations, and they certainly advocate the judicious use of audio-visual aids.

The use of the media then can be based on sound argument and supported by expert opinion. But cases can be lost by overstating them. We should be aware that less rational, though not necessarily less legitimate, processes are at work. It is not just the calculated question about what will be most effective. It is also a feeling for and sharing in the ethos of the times. Here we see the Liturgy taking on the colour of its surroundings. That is not improper as we shall argue later but it is a slippery process, harder to tie down or justify in terms of reasoned argument. It is all the more important therefore to recognise this variation for what it is and to realise how much it owes to our contemporary culture.

In one sense that is perfectly obvious. One can hardly be present at an act of worship where liberal use is made of film projectors, tape recorders and various other machines without being aware of the technological prowess of the age. Many of the options were not open to our predecessors. But there is a less obvious sense in which multi-media worship is a child of its time and here we turn to the first of our two characteristics.

It is noticeable that many of the media shy away from the use of words. We will dance, dramatise, mimic, touch, look at pictures, march, listen to music, even remain silent rather than speak. Such reticence is understandable in an age for which words seem to have become even more problematical than usual. The reasons why that should be so are not easy to tie down. Is it that there are simply too many of them? Has the coinage been devalued by its ready availability through the press and mass communication systems? Do politicians find it difficult to keep their words and are they always having to eat them mainly because they are expected to produce so many for consumption by vast numbers of people? In these circumstances it is not surprising that 'by their deeds you shall know them' begins to sound like a more reliable guide.

There may be other reasons for our scepticism although they are rarely if ever articulated by most of us. We are scarcely aware of them. The philosophers for instance have been busy analysing language and asking awkward questions about what it means. They have doubted whether some of it, including the language of faith, means anything at all! If their original onslaught has been significantly modified, the unsettling effect remains and makes many of us guard our tongues. It is also worth remembering that words do not have meaning in themselves so much as gain their meaning from the way in which they are used and from the whole context of shared ideas in which they are set. These shared ideas are harder to come by in a time of transition when old and stable patterns have broken up and we not only face continuous changes in our physical surroundings, social customs and ways of life, but lack a common way of understanding ourselves and of thinking about our world. It may be a long time before we find such a community of ideas again, and in circumstances such as these it can be hard to talk to one another.

In addition there is growing dissatisfaction with the way our society, not least in religious affairs, has exalted the rational and intellectual life of man, where words are his stock in trade, to the detriment of other aspects of his personality. This is one aspect of our disenchantment with the tidy gods of a rather hard-headed culture where the clear and calculated are at a premium and mystery is at a discount. A more than passing interest in the traditions of the East, in transcendental meditation, in drugs and psychedelic experience no less than the desire to make music, to dream and dance, to touch and trust the subjective world of one's inner feelings are inevitably anti-intellectual in tone but can be appreciated as the reassertion of important but neglected aspects of human nature.

One cannot help wondering if a good deal of the significance of Pentecostalism, not as a denomination but as a dimension of Christian experience in all denominations, is to be understood along these lines. May it not be the counter-culture in liturgical terms? It certainly places a welcome emphasis on the more spontaneous, uninhibited, intuitive and emotional levels of experience. It has long embraced the less technological aspects of multi-media worship. And what is to be made of the phenomenon of speaking in tongues in the context of our self-consciousness over words? Those who have grown slow of speech, not through any lack of intellectual skills but through becoming over concerned with them, may find in this inarticulate groaning a language without words to express what seems to have become too difficult for words, or is quite simply beyond them.

Factors such as these may begin to explain why we shy away from words in multi-media worship and look for other ways to express what we feel and experience. It ought to be made clear that explanations do not imply uncritical approval. To counteract an over-emphasis on the intellect should not amount to a first move towards despising it. To recognise our difficulties over words is not to deny that they are the highest form of communication known to man. An appreciation of some aspects of Pentecostalism need not cloud our judgement about its excesses. The need to try to talk sense still remains.

Whilst looking at the influence of culture on the Liturgy, it is interesting to speculate about an earlier transition from highly ceremonious worship to the increasing domination of words which stems from the Reformation period and is still with us in many traditional patterns of worship today. More than one factor was at work but it is possible that when printing gave rise to the spread of books and more and more people learned how to read, many of the old movements and gestures in the Liturgy began to seem super-fluous. Ceremony was a clumsy form of communication in the new age of literacy. Then as now the change in worship reflected a more general change in the culture of society at large.

All these considerations add weight to the warning that multi-media worship should not be caught out thinking more highly of itself than it ought to think. If it is something of a cultural phe-nomenon; it may also be a passing one. It is none the worse for that, but if we can envisage an age which recovers its confidence in words, even if they are different and its language more reticent, we should be careful not to regard multi-media worship as an unquestionable norm.

In some ways the first characteristic has turned out to be a rather negative rebellion against the monopoly of words in worship, but it has positive results. It is a move in the right direction. It encourages a more rounded expression of the sort of beings we are. It does not however quite make us all-rounders. The wholeness of man must take account not only of the mind, feelings, instincts and the like, but of the body as well.

Here we turn to the second characteristic of multi-media worship, namely a positive attitude to the material world showing itself in an uninhibited use of all kinds of material things and a much wider variety of physical activity. A glance at the examples referred to at the beginning of this section reveals a full range of sensory experience. People touch, see, hear, smell and when sharing bread and wine, taste as well. They have plenty of opportunity to move about. They are encouraged to make use of their bodies.

This pride in the things of the earth and in being part of the earth appears to say something about convictions as well as about cultural trends. A theological factor is at work. The insight is not a new one but corresponds to an emphasis deep-seated within the Christian tradition.

The Bible and the long experience of the church offer it a good deal of support. More often than not Christians have made use of silver and gold, jewels and fine cloth, wood and glass, pictures and books, sculpture and symbols for the business of the Liturgy, not to mention the bread and the wine at the heart of it. They have knelt for prayers, stood for the Gospel, savoured the incense, observed the ceremonies, gone in procession, feasted their eyes on colour and splendour, exchanged the kiss of peace. Even dancing is not unknown though admittedly it was frequently under attack.

The rites of the Eastern Orthodox churches have long had most of what it takes to qualify as multi-media worship. The comings and goings between the sanctuary and the nave from one side of the screen (iconostasis) to the other with the opening and closing of doors and the veiling of the holy table provided plenty of drama and movement; and that is not to mention the pictures on the walls, the liberal use of incense, the vestments of the priests, the lights, the carrying of cross, scourge, thorns and spear, and the kissing of ikons and the book of the Gospel. Much the same could be said of the Western Mass with its Gallican embroidery including bellringing, genuflexions, censing and a great deal of ceremony.

The reasons why the Liturgy has often taken such delight in the physical world and the bodily existence of man are complex. In the East, as we have already seen, they include a profound awareness that the so-called material world is inter-penetrated with less immediately obvious realities, and to this awareness we shall return. For the present we need only underline a straightforward and oft-repeated affirmation, and that is that the material world which includes the human body is fundamentally good.

To talk in terms of material things and spiritual things is sometimes a way of making useful distinctions although the line between them is by no means as clear as is often supposed and in the end is probably non-existent. Hebrew thought however, which has greatly influenced Christian thought, regarded it as a mistake to turn this familiar distinction into a value judgement by suggesting that matter is evil whilst spirit is good or that God is interested in one and not in the other. Both are good. Both are capable of corruption and misuse, but according to Christian belief both have a future and are open to being made new. These convictions shine through at any number of points. The first chapter of the Bible for example is not to be understood as a prosaic description of the grand opening of the world but as a lyrical affirmation that everything owes its existence to God who was pleased with what he had made. It may have been used in worship since the recurring refrain suggests a congregational response: "And God saw that it was good." Many of the Psalms take up the theme. The doctrine of the Incarnation suggests among other things that God is most clearly revealed in terms of the bodily existence of a human being. The Word was made flesh. For Paul the spiritual man is not a man who despises the material world, but a man whose whole life, body and soul, is lived in a restored relationship to God through Christ. Such views were sympathetic to the Hebraic insight now confirmed by our present understanding of man as a psycho-physical organism. Everything is interrelated with everything else and you cannot finally divide people up into separate parts. To believe in the Resurrection of the Body rather than the Immortality of the Soul is to believe that the person as a whole will die and be made alive rather than that the physical body will die whilst the soul survives the grave. If the latter were true then the soul is not only distinct from the body but spirit emerges triumphant over matter in an endless game of one-upmanship. The Christian vision thinks otherwise and looks forward to a new heaven and a new earth and One who makes all things new.

The assumption all along is that matter, including the human body, is not to be despised and this positive approach is clear for all to see in multi-media worship. We might almost call it a full-blooded approach as far as the worshippers are concerned. They are no longer reduced to listeners who occasionally burst into song and stretch their legs as if too wide a range of sensory experience were inappropriate. They no longer behave as if they were half ashamed of what in fact they are, beings of flesh and blood who look and see and listen not only in limited ways but in many ways and do many other things as well. In fact these forms of worship are often genuinely

89

avant-garde in offering a rounded expression of man's being which is less impoverished than his truncated experience in the everyday world; and what better compliment could be paid to those who tell a Story which claims to offer men life in all its fullness?

Multi-media worship then, apart from what it owes to technological progress, is not entirely new, neither is it alien to the biblical insight that since this is God's world everything in it is fundamentally good. But although this affirmative approach is not without solid support, it would be misleading to give the impression that there is absolute unanimity between Christians, even the very early ones. They have often been in two minds on the subject. There is disagreement as to whether material things including the human body are fundamentally good or important after all. The contrary opinion owes something to the influence of Greek ideas which regarded the soul as the prisoner of the body longing to be free, and matter as secondary to spirit, and this world as but a pale shadow of the real world. Opposed to the Hebrew outlook, these ideas have vied with it in Christian thought from the very beginning.

Perhaps a more important contributor to disagreement has been everybody's experience of life in the body. It is such an ambiguous affair. It can be full of occasions of enjoyment and pleasure and the sense of physical well being. It can equally be marred by pain and misery. If the world is God's responsibility then out of universal and often bitter experience we must add that it is a very heavy one. It is not surprising that man has often felt that his only release was to get away from it if he could, but in any case to deny it as evil rather than affirm it as good. Multi-media worship is not likely to commend itself to people who tend to think and feel this way.

Before leaving the subject we ought finally to note that multi-media worship has failed to commend itself in particular to a good many people in the Protestant churches since the Reformation, indeed we frequently come across trends which are the very reverse of the two characteristics we have mentioned. Far from words being put into second place they have something of a field day; and the Liturgy becomes austere as it grows suspicious of the things of this world.

The wordiness of post-Reformation worship, sometimes amounting to verbosity, owed a great deal to a renewed and welcome emphasis on the Word of God in Scripture. No service was complete without a sermon. In Calvin's Geneva people talked about 'going to the sermon' rather than 'going to Mass', and in England the Puritan preacher often spoke for an hour as a dying man to dying men. Words were the bearers of salvation and negligence could mean souls condemned to hell.

Coupled with this emphasis on preaching was the desire to teach the truths of the Christian faith and make sure that people understood. Luther felt deeply the need for informed minds and trained consciences. He tended to turn the Liturgy into an educational exercise, and the opportunities for instruction were not limited to the sermon. The prayers, especially in Calvin's Liturgy, became extremely long and didactic in tone. It was easy to gain the impression that they were composed more for the benefit of the congregation than for the ears of God.

In the case of Calvin and his heirs, the English Puritans, the renewed emphasis on Scripture also led to a crusade against many of the external features of the Liturgy. The Bible was now regarded as authoritative not only in doctrinal matters but in matters of liturgical procedure as well. If Luther had retained all that was not clearly contrary to Scripture, the more radical Calvin was of the opinion that worship should only contain what Scripture specifically recommended, and Puritan prayer books, following his rule, contain interesting marginal notes quoting scriptural texts in support of quite minor details.

We have already indicated that we regard the Bible as a crucial check point for worship but not as a source of explicit instructions and therefore welcome this renewed respect for Scripture whilst criticising the way in which it was used. The result however was that as a matter of principle prayer, praise, preaching, the Lord's Supper, the Psalms and the Lord's Prayer were in, whilst ceremonies, ornaments, vestments, genuflexions, signs of the cross and the like were out. In some cases even organs and responsive prayers were disallowed.

But the increasing austerity of post-Reformation worship also reveals an indifference to the material world which was out of sympathy with Hebrew ways of thought. Zwingli for example was not only anxious to make sure that everyone worshipped with an understanding mind, he seemed to imply that the mind was all that mattered. He did not don the scholar's gown like Luther but wore the everyday clothes of a leading member of the community. This was not an attempt to integrate the Liturgy with ordinary life, an attempt which we might well applaud, but a demonstration of what little value he placed on such outward things at all. Even the Lord's Supper, which deals so unashamedly with matter, was to be understood (or misunderstood) in the light of John 6.63 which was read at every service: "It is the spirit which quickeneth, the flesh profiteth nothing."

Similarly Calvin, for all his emphasis on the unity of Word and Sacrament denied the sacramental principle which holds that things like bread and wine are suffused with spiritual reality and the material world is the bearer of the divine presence. For Calvin the gracious activity of God by-passed the loaf and the cup to deal directly with the human heart. They remain only as props made necessary by the weakness of faith. They have no essential part to play. Logically they can be dispensed with and, as communion became increasingly infrequent, it seemed that logic, amongst other things, had won the day.

Not all Reformation Liturgies were plain. Luther, probably out of conservatism rather than conviction, perpetuated a form of worship which horrified some of his contemporaries because it looked for all the world like the Mediaeval Mass. But there remains much in the Protestant tradition which is quite alien to the spirit of multi-media worship. We have talked about some of the causes. Perhaps the main one has still to be reckoned with and that was the excesses of the Mediaeval Mass which forced the Reformers to protest in an effort to restore the purity of Christian worship. Maybe it was this understandable reaction as much as any unsatisfactory views about matter and spirit, or any disenchantment with the things of this world, or any application of a rather dubious principle of liturgical reform, which gave rise to the exceedingly plain and simple forms of worship which were to follow.

The Puritans, with their white-washed meeting houses and their services which offered virtually nothing to see and nothing to do, stand in history as timely reminders of the dangers open to the ceremonious kind of worship represented by the Mediaeval Mass and, in our day, by the multi-media Liturgy.

Apart from its unsavoury views about sacrifice, in the opinion of the Reformers the Mass had increasingly neglected the Word. The lessons were brief and more often than not the sermon was non-existent. Quite apart from the church's duty to announce the good news of the Gospel, the level of its understanding must always be at risk if it neglects to organise its faith into speech. There is a modern counterpart to this neglect when, for example, the means of communication begin to count for more than what it is that has to be communicated, and the communicator does not agonise over what he has to say as much as how he plans to 'say' it. Of course the medium is a message about the goodness of the created world, but the particular message of the Christian Story can become unduly subordinate to a multitude of media. It may be just as serious as failing to preach the Word altogether if words which seemed unable to carry authentic meanings are now replaced by sights and sounds and experiences which carry little coherent meaning at all.

Again in the opinion of the Reformers the Mass had become over concerned with externals so that it began to look like an outside without an inside as if all the ceremony had lost heart or taken leave of its senses. A contemporary ritualism could likewise develop by paying more attention to what is being done or used than to what we are doing or using it for. Excess is perhaps the wrong word to describe the misuse of material things. It is not a question of going too far. We cannot have too much of them and they are not to be spurned in favour of a more refined and spiritual world. But a light touch on the surface will not do when we are invited to feel their sacramental texture. The danger is not one of taking matter and bodies too seriously but of not taking them seriously enough as bearers and sharers in the glory of an "everlasting world perpetually at work" (Edwin Muir).

There is a great deal that is valuable in multi-media worship, especially in its more rounded not to say wholesome view of man. For most of us this is not the moment to steer clear of it but to be more energetic in pursuit of its objectives. But we must keep a sense of proportion and not provoke another and equally justifiable puritan reaction. We can make too much of multi-media worship. We could become mere followers of fashion. It is certainly a lighter thing than the question of relevance, to which we now turn.

Down-to-earth

On examination, the demand that worship should be relevant reveals a number of rather different concerns. Some have been touched on already; others not only owe something to the contemporary mood but reflect current dissatisfaction with the institutional church. Since worship remains its most distinctive activity it is not surprising when it becomes a focus for criticism. We will look briefly at two examples.

First, there is an impatience with any call to worship whatever, and one suspects it might remain even when the Liturgy has been refashioned to the best of our ability. Are there not better and more

93

relevant things to do, and would not the time be better spent alongside other people tackling something really worthwhile like the innumerable social problems that face us all? Service rather than services might be the order of the day. This is an understandable reaction to a church which appears to be over pre-occupied with its own religious affairs and internal problems, when its energies ought to be re-directed elsewhere.

The implied criticism is justified but it ought to be set alongside another which is equally to the point. A cult of activism flourishes in certain sections of our society. Christians are not the least of its devotees. Their arrangements are difficult to make because their diaries are so full. People complain about being busy as if nothing more need be said to justify their existence. It is those with time to stare who are suspect. If more of us did just that we might realise that a good deal of what we do might be better left undone. Perhaps that is why we keep going. But however praiseworthy our pursuits, occasionally we need to call a halt. It is essential to stop and think. The Liturgy ought never to be an escape or a substitute for action, but it does have something to do with this need to stand back quite consciously from what we are doing, uncover the sources of our inspiration and regain a sense of perspective. Detachment is required of us no less than involvement.

Second, the current reputation of the church for ineffectiveness inevitably rubs off on the Liturgy. It is irrelevant because it is hard to see what it achieves. Again the point should be taken. A church which makes little difference to the life of the community should come in for criticism, and that is not to fall for any simple criterion of its success. Likewise a Liturgy which apparently does little to improve the church has no cause for complacency. Not that there is anything automatic about it. The most adequate diet of worship will not inevitably result in a healthy church any more than a healthy church will inevitably result in a redeemed society. People remain free to choose. But there is a longstanding tradition which expects the Liturgy to be a means whereby the Christian community is broken and remade, cleansed and renewed, brought repeatedly under the gracious judgement and healing of the Story and invigorated by the spirit of Jesus. Paul was concerned, in 1 Corinthians 14.26, that everything should be done to build up the body of Christ.

In agreeing that worship ought to achieve something we should be wary of the thirst for immediate results. Relevance should not be equated with what is regarded as immediately useful—a common

94

mistake in more than one area of life. The Liturgy is not a source of instant solutions and it is not likely to change the church overnight. Its most valuable work will be done in persistently nourishing the life of the community, building up attitudes, increasing sensitivities, recreating visions and perspectives, forming persons and relationships which will provide resources for living which are not easily exhausted just as they are not easily identified.

But in accepting the criticism that the Liturgy often achieves all too little we must criticise the popular notion that everything is to be judged by its usefulness. If it is to be worthwhile it must produce tangible results. Having done it you must have something to show for it. It must measure up to the technocrat's demand for efficiency.

Such criteria, useful on many occasions, ignore a whole range of human activities of which it is more accurate to say that we do them for their own sake than with any ulterior motive in mind. Like man himself they are better understood as ends in themselves rather than as means to an end. They are valued for what they are, not for what they can achieve. Here is the realm of play rather than of work, and of games, festivity and fun. A celebration of an anniversary or a piece of good fortune is never thought of as achieving anything beyond the expression of our delight that such things are there to be celebrated. In similar vein, human relations are at their worst when people are used and at their best when we simply enjoy one another's company. It is conceivable that we may wish to celebrate the Story of Jesus for its own sake, as a sign of our profound pleasure that it exists to be told and without any thought of what might be achieved by so doing. None of this is useful beyond the fact that it is useless and that this sort of uselessness has an essential place in human life.

Here then are two kinds of irrelevance which represent justifiable criticisms of the church, but in so far as they reflect the temper of our times, they are by no means beyond questioning.

A third example of irrelevance is another aspect of the second since again it is concerned about the effects of the Liturgy, but this time on those who take part. We shall deal later with the complaint that it seems remote from everyday concerns. We look now at the complaint that it doesn't meet people's needs. It is irrelevant because it doesn't do anything for me. I don't go away with a sense of forgiveness or renewal. My sickness is not made well. My spirit is not refreshed. It doesn't help me to cope with life. I go out of habit or a sense of duty, but afterwards I don't feel any better than before.

One source of confusion should be removed at the start. Our

feelings are important and we should respect them, but they are not always a sure guide to how things actually are. People often feel they have done badly when they have done well and vice versa. We often feel very low when in fact the worst is over and we are on the way to a full recovery. Experiences that are unpleasant or just plain dull can be good for us. The Liturgy may not always be exciting. It may sometimes be disturbing. We may well feel depressed when it is over, but that is not necessarily an indication that nothing has been achieved. Feelings are notoriously unreliable.

That is not however the main point that people make, and when they make it they usually come in for some severe criticism. "You do not worship" we are told "for what you can get out of it." "You go to make an offering not to get a blessing!" If that warns us against going to the Liturgy merely for our own sakes, the warning is justified. It is inevitable of course that as human beings that is partly what we shall do, but it is also possible that we shall ask for blessing so that we shall be a blessing and in us "all the families of the earth will be blessed" (Genesis 12.3).

If the rebuke means that we ought not to go to get a blessing at all, and should not expect the Liturgy to meet our needs in any way, that is clearly nonsense. Those who are dissatisfied with worship because it is itself unsatisfying cannot be put off by being told they have misunderstood, as if the Story of Jesus, however much we celebrate if for its own sake, had nothing to do with meeting the needs of those who tell it. If that is not in some sense true it is hard to see why it was ever told. In any case, for many of the story tellers it reveals a God who, contrary to what had often been thought, is on man's side and is busy at work on his behalf. Just as the Sabbath is made for man and not man for the Sabbath, so it appears are many other things, and there is a strong suspicion that if Jesus is characteristically a man for others he reveals a God who also exists for man. The whole business is humane and it would be strange if the result were to be a Liturgy in which God is worshipped or finds any pleasure in being glorified at the expense of his creatures, as if his glorification were in inverse proportion to the diminishment of man.

We have every right to go to the Liturgy fully expecting that it will meet our needs and we are equally right to grow uneasy if it turns out not to be the case in any sense. What is mistaken is to think those needs will be met by concentrating on them over much. We come with our own and the world's troubles, failures, fears, perversions and anxieties, disappointments, wounds and sorrows all packaged in big words like 'evil' and 'sin'. We are more than likely to go away as we came if they remain our chief pre-occupation and we endlessly confess our faults, analyse our problems and brood over our troubles as if by introspection and effort we shall of ourselves generate new and better states of mind and so go home feeling it has all been worthwhile. This is so-called subjective worship. Its ancestry can be traced back at least as far as the Middle Ages when the unfortunate developments we noted earlier (see pages 59–62) not only drove the laity out of the Liturgy but, with nothing better to do, turned them in upon themselves. The Reformers, who were the children as well as the scourge of the mediaeval church, inherited these subjective tendencies and they have been with us ever since. Many a hymn book gives itself away by the disproportionate amount of space allotted to hymns about ourselves rather than about the events concerning Jesus and the adoration of God; and many a sermon betrays a similar subjectivism by having much more to say about what we must do for God than what God has done for us.

These subjective tendencies are self-defeating. The realities of life should not be overlooked, but if they are to be dealt with creatively, which is not the same as solving all our problems, new resources are required. We need help from outside. Our stories are renewed by the Story.

Some of the wisest forms of worship have remembered this, and one suspects that a major reason why ours become arid is because we forget it. The Daily Office (see page 2) which has come down to us in the form of Morning and Evening Prayer, is not the Liturgy as we have already said. It was probably consciously intended to strengthen the life of those who took part. It was supposed to do you good, but it set about it by drawing the worshipper out of himself into a rigorous and disciplined recital of the Psalms and a systematic reading of the Bible, all done with meticulous care as an offering to God. It had objective strength. Likewise the Liturgy which was so misused in the Middle Ages had distinctly better possibilities. When the Gallican and Roman traditions were combined in the Western synthesis to give us the basis of the Roman Mass as we know it today, their distinctive contributions helped to overcome in each other their separate weaknesses. At worship the Gallicans were very much aware of themselves, the ugliness and cruelty of the world about them and their own sins and temptations. Their pessimistic mood and their longing for release pervade the Liturgy. But there is a certain human warmth in contrast to the colder austerity of the

Roman rite. This paid less attention to how the worshippers were feeling and concentrated on the business in hand. The people had come to do the actions of the Liturgy, to offer, give thanks, break and share. In so doing their minds were kept on the sacrifice of Christ and were not encouraged to wander elsewhere. The Eastern rite, like the Roman, does not dwell on people's problems. The secret of its recreative power is to draw the worshippers out of themselves into the drama of God's redemptive activity.

Without denying the realities of life or their importance we need to be distracted from ourselves to something greater and more hopeful. This is one good reason for using the lectionary (see page 18) in the first part of the Liturgy as well as keeping closely to the four actions in the second. It is natural to turn to passages in the Bible that seem to speak to our particular concerns and meet our needs, but the end result could easily be a somewhat narrow selection of readings, making Jesus too much in the image of our immediate problems. Vast tracts of the Bible, and with them important and rewarding aspects of the Christian tradition may be ignored. This is not to commend the indiscriminate reading of Scripture but an overall rather than a partial view and a principle of selection based on something other than personal preference. We do not choose food simply to suit our taste but to provide a balanced and nourishing diet.

In all this a note of irrelevance will be struck. We shall be invited to consider matters which may have little to do with the things we want to talk about the most. Our attention is distracted. Such irrelevance reminds us of the givenness of the faith. It is not merely the product of our own reflections on our own experiences. It comes to break up the old arrangements, transcend the sensible considerations which seem of first importance when we get immersed in practicalities. It goes beyond the obvious possibilities. It strikes a foreign note. Something is added to the situations in which we find ourselves, even if it is no more than a very odd and provocative story. Its extraordinary character is set alongside our present condition. The two are not easily related nor the tension between them resolved, but the imagination may be stimulated to see visions and dream dreams of new men and new worlds. At first sight these may be 'way out', totally irrelevant and easily dismissed as sheer fantasy, but they are more important to us and more creative than we often realise.

Such irrelevance is the friend of objectivity. It is the other side of the same coin, and the Liturgy's insistence on not always talking about what we want to talk about will in the long run do us more good than paying too much attention to our own tales of woe.

But if objectivity is so profitable what has become of our earlier recognition of the importance of doing the Liturgy for its own sake and not for utilitarian purposes? To use more traditional language, is not God to be worshipped as an end in himself and not as a means to an end, and is not the chief end of man to glorify God and enjoy him for ever? Without denying the disinterested nature of true worship, we need to add a rider. To glorify God in self-forgetfulness is not in the final resort an unrewarding activity. We have every reason to believe it can be a very costly one and, left to ourselves, impossible to achieve without becoming calculating and therefore self-defeating, but as a matter of fact, or rather of faith, it is where human fulfilment is to be found.

As to the possible charge that we are in danger of reducing the Liturgy to a dubious therapeutic technique, we should be wary of the technique but unapologetic about the therapy. We do not discredit the Liturgy by regarding it as a source of well-being. We honour it. Far from dissuading people from going "to get a blessing" one hopes to see them caught up in an activity so reminiscent of certain extraordinary goings-on that occasionally the godspell is cast and they disperse with the distinct impression that part of them or the whole of them, not finally, but for the time being is risen from the dead.

We have looked at irrelevance in the sense that there are more relevant or better things to do than attend church services and in the sense that the Liturgy is ineffective in building up the church and in meeting the needs of those who take part. We turn now to the more basic complaint that worship is irrelevant because it exists in a world of its own which has little if anything to do with the world in which we live. The two are virtually in separate compartments. The real pursuits of the work-a-day world receive scarcely any attention in the Sunday service and, for all the encouragement we receive to take our Christianity into daily life, what we hear about in church is notoriously difficult to relate in any meaningful way to the realities of the world from which we came.

The complaint can easily be exaggerated. There can be few acts of worship where, in prayers of confession or prayers for others or in preaching, the facts of life don't at least make their presence felt. More often it is not that all of life is left unmentioned by some conspiracy of silence but that we are highly selective as to what is mentioned and what is ignored. The Liturgy takes notice of rather restricted areas. It is more likely to take notice for example of home and family than of economic and political affairs, of the 'respectable' sins than the seamier side of life, of weakness and need than of what men are frankly proud of, of the natural order rather than the highly artificial, to name but a few. If this does not amount to a world apart it adds up to the impression of a world rather different from the one we live in. We are even urged at times to put that world out of our minds for an hour or so, not for the sake of objectivity, for which we've recently cast a vote, but to forget about mundane affairs altogether.

These and other tendencies give rise to the suspicion that the Liturgy is irrelevant and has little to do with life as we know it. This is something more than an impatience with the Bible because it holds rather old-fashioned views, or worse, has no views at all about many of the things that interest us. That kind of irrelevance may be inconvenient but it need not be a problem if we make an intelligent approach to a highly significant but very ancient piece of literature. The irrelevance that concerns us does not simply come with age. It is more like the person who through illness or laziness or fear ceases to go out and about anymore, and because he has withdrawn and lost all kinds of contacts rapidly becomes out of touch.

Without going back on our conviction that we should not be over pre-occupied with our immediate concerns when we do the Liturgy together, we must go on to give reasons why we must nevertheless remain firmly in touch with life, and indicate ways in which this kind of relatedness or relevance can be maintained.

The first reason why the Liturgy must be down-to-earth and in touch with life takes us back to the beginning of our whole discussion, where we looked at some permanent features of this central and distinctive act of Christian worship. We noted the basic pattern of Word and Sacrament and suggested that its central concern was to tell the Story and so affirm that its hero, Jesus of Nazareth, and the events concerning him "have supreme *worth* or significance for our lives".

This last phrase (see page 27) suggests that the kind of relevance we are now talking about is fundamental to our whole understanding of the Liturgy. It belongs not to the variables but to the essentials. The fact that Christians repeatedly do the Liturgy together and have done so for centuries is their way of underlining the importance of the Story that lies embedded within it. They proclaim its worth by becoming obsessional storytellers. But it cannot be important in a vacuum. It cannot matter so much and be irrelevant at the same time. It has worth or importance precisely because it has such significance for our lives. It strikes us as uniquely revealing. It throws a flood of light on what life is about. It opens our eyes to truth and goodness and beauty and the ways in which they are being achieved through love and sacrifice, death and resurrection. It is unsurpassed as an interpretative tool and a source for understanding what is going on in the world within and around us. To allow the Liturgy to lose contact with life is to refute the fundamental affirmation about the significance of the Story. Christian worship denies itself when it grows out of touch. X-ray equipment is no use left in the cupboard and we shall not take seriously the claims that are made for it unless it is brought out and used for investigations.

But if we are dealing here with essentials we shall not expect variety to be very far behind. Not everyone will necessarily agree about what the investigations reveal. One opinion may differ from another. Some may conclude, however reluctantly, that the case is a write-off, whilst others may insist that matters are not beyond repair. In the history of the church for example there has always been a certain amount of tension between what is referred to as a 'this-worldly' and an 'other-worldly' approach to faith and worship and it is not likely to be resolved. We noticed its presence in the differences between worship in the East with its intimations of immortality and in the West where the changeable features of time are allowed to intrude much more.

Perhaps in the early days of Christianity other-worldliness did arise out of a lack of conviction about the Story having much significance for life simply because this life had little significance. The early church looked forward to the imminent return of Christ. It was just about all over. Their ethics were emergency regulations. Their faith and worship had a strong eschatological emphasis. They were not concerned with time but with the end (eschatos) of time and they regarded the end as near. Bitterly persecuted they felt that they didn't belong here and they wouldn't be here long. Small wonder if they had no qualms about allowing their Liturgies to lose contact with the world about them. It was only when the years dragged on and the end did not come as expected that the church had to make a radical readjustment. Christ was now the final clue which gives away the plot in the middle of the play but he was not the last act before the curtain falls and the show is over. They had to settle down to life in this world.

Since then, if other-worldliness persists it is not the result of simply dismissing any suggestion that the Story is relevant to life, and keeping the X-ray equipment in the cupboard. Rather it is one of the conclusions people come to when, true to our insistence on its relevance, the Story is brought to bear on our worldly experience. We are not inclined these days to write it off. On the whole we are favourably disposed towards a this-worldly emphasis. But we should take account of the important notes which are sounded by an other-worldly approach. It is a constant reminder that however much we value the world as God's responsibility and therefore as fundamentally good, it still leaves much to be desired and requires of us a large measure of critical detachment. In addition it reminds us that although we believe that the world really matters and is to be experienced and not merely survived, we do not believe that it exhausts reality. There is more to be said, and if we have to settle down and deal with it seriously, we also suspect that our living is not the whole of the enterprise and our dying does not amount to journey's end. We are not yet at home. The image of ourselves as strangers and pilgrims is hard to resist. Our eyes must be in two places at once: on the ground and looking to the future.

Such insights will turn back and have their effect on the Liturgy. Where in the light of experience they become unusually intense, it may well become an austere and world-denying affair. Others, in other times and places, may come to rather different conclusions, and turn that same Liturgy into a celebration of a myriad facets of this-worldly existence.

But these emphases should always be the result of the interplay between faith and life which is demanded by the Christian claim that the Story is important for us. Unless we tell the Story and do the Liturgy somewhere in the midst of our life and not in isolation from it, it is impossible to insist on its significance or to discover what conclusions should be reached in the light of it. We shall not know what it is about life in this world which can be affirmed and what should be denied, where we can say 'Yes' and where we must say 'No' unless Liturgy and life are constantly forced to confront each other. This is the fundamental reason for welcoming those forms of the Liturgy where, once the basic pattern is secured, the sounds of this world are mingled with the sounds of the Story that is told, for only in so doing is there any likelihood of distinguishing between discord and harmony and of discerning that resonance which is common to both.

To proclaim the Story as significant is to boast about its relevance and to want to surround it with life. To proclaim it as significant and then to relegate it to the role of a museum piece or a curio is a contradiction in terms.

The second reason why the Liturgy must be firmly in touch with life involves us in an escalation of our understanding of the Liturgy itself. In discussing it to date we have not ventured far beyond the minimal requirements for joining in. If people regard its Story as of fundamental importance, so much so that they wish to commit themselves to telling it over and over again, then they are welcome to do so as members of the Christian community. Jesus for them is Lord and that is the essential Christian confession. They may or may not wish to bring God into it, but if they do, then the Liturgy becomes something more than a story time. The events which involved and centred around Jesus of Nazareth are regarded by the majority of Christians as a unique revelation of the character and pursuits of God. In them he is seen at work as never before or since. The Liturgy focuses attention on what he did there for man in a Christlike way. It casts wondering eyes on his creative living, suffering and dying. It not only observes these things very closely but honours them and couples with its profound admiration and respect an enthusiastic vote of gratitude. Such is the adoration, praise and thanksgiving of worship.

But is this God only encountered in the Story of Jesus, and is celebrating his activity merely a matter of reminiscing about the past? Here we come back to the way in which theology changes and in turn affects our worship. The concern to bring worship down-to-earth owes a good deal to contemporary thinking about God which, as we have said before, is not so much a novelty as a recovery of neglected insights. If some find it difficult to talk about him at all, most wish to go on doing so but in a different way. It is not that his character has changed. He is still the Christlike God we have seen in Jesus and we believe he always will be, but there is something more to be said and at this point we wish to put things rather differently.

If we describe our contemporary image of God by way of contrast it is not in order to caricature someone else's views, but to clarify our own. For at least three hundred years in the Western part of the world we can trace something of an argument between two ideas. The first regarded God as virtually outside of the world. He was 'up there'. He was transcendent because he was distant and faraway. To find him you must turn, as it were, from mundane realities and look elsewhere. The second view, regards God as being very much down-to-earth. He is still transcendent but by being different from everything else rather than distant. The first view, taken to extremes, found it difficult to allow God to make his presence felt in the world at all. He had made it, as an engineer makes a machine, and having set it going left it to run its course. God's presence was something of an interference which interrupted the normal course of events. The supreme example would be his intrusion in the person of Jesus Christ. The other view does not think of God as one who makes occasional sorties into the world but believes he is present and active all the time, thoroughly mixed up in worldly affairs. He is not even a constant interruption but part of the scene. He is not here today and gone tomorrow but continuously involved in the ongoing story of the universe.

No limits are set to this involvement. That does not mean that everything equals God. That is the mistake we call 'pantheism'. It does mean that God is in everything. It is misleading to locate him in the religious for example but not in the secular or in the extraordinary but not the unremarkable. It is impossible to move out of his territory. All is sacred in the sense that he is active everywhere and all the time struggling with men towards the humane goals we have glimpsed in Christ.

This second view of God finds increasing favour and it implies a rather different attitude to the world about us. We must take it very seriously if it is the arena of God's activity, and we must regard it less superficially than we have been encouraged to do in the past. A pseudo-scientific approach has tended to trust only the surface of things—what we came to regard as hard facts, the things we could touch and see in the most obvious world of sensible experience. Now we are increasingly aware that the more we examine this world the more mystery we find. There is much more to it than meets the eye. There are realities beyond appearances. Just as people cannot be reduced to biological, chemical or even psychological descriptions, important as they may be, so the world cannot be reduced to its analysable parts. There is more and it is not so easily tied down. Those who believe in God would wish to say that it is a sacramental universe and that part of its mystery is his dynamic presence within the fabric of life, constantly at work in a Christlike way to bring man and his world to fulfilment. "Lift the stone and you will find me, cleave the wood and I am there."

If such views are at all acceptable it will mean that we do not expect to meet God by turning away from the experiences of life and our everyday encounters with other people but by doing the very opposite, regarding them with even greater interest and open to their latent possibilities.

There is an important distinction to be kept clear at this point. It cannot be denied that most people need to withdraw from time to time from the business of living. The fact of sleep, the day off, the desire to be alone, the occasional night on the tiles, the refreshment found in art and literature, the appreciation of contemplative silence all witness to this reality. The need to withdraw, even to forget, is not in question. The mistake is made when we go on to say that we need that kind of withdrawal and forgetfulness in order to be with God, so that detachment becomes something more than a necessary counterbalance to involvement, as sleep is to waking and relaxation is to effort. It implies that God is to be found elsewhere than in our everyday world and, according to our way of thinking, that is not the case.

Since God is among us, when the Liturgy celebrates his activity it cannot confine its attentions to the ethereal or to the past. It will be interested in what he is up to now, and it must be in touch with life because that is where he is busy at work. No one will pretend that his activity is easy to see, any more than it was in Palestine 2,000 years ago. What took place was in many ways outstanding, but it was so genuinely a part of the mundane affairs of that restless little country that it didn't occur to most people that it was divine activity at all. Then as now it is easily overlooked. He was, and still is in the world, but men do not recognise his incarnate presence.

Our attempts to do so and the conclusions we come to will add another dimension to our preaching, whatever form it eventually takes. So far we have seen it mainly as part of the business of rehearsing those events to which our faith is a response, though it will be impossible to separate that from saying something about their meaning and implications. If in addition we believe them to be revealing about the activity of God we shall go on to understand preaching as a proclamation of what God has done for man in Jesus. To leave it there would be infinitely preferable to many familiar and inadequate substitutes (see page 18). Clearly there is room for other sermons at other times just as there is room for other services, but in the Liturgy we should be careful to stick to the point.

There remains a further dimension. If we have confidence that the

God who was at work in Jesus is at work in the world today, then we shall want to open men's eyes to any signs of his gracious presence in our contemporary experience. Our proclamation of this good news will need to be hedged around with a great deal of modesty and self-awareness. It is all too easy to masquerade our own prejudices as God's business, and at best we can say no more than what seems to us to be his way in the world in the light of what we know of him already in the Bible and the long reflective processes of the church. This proclamation will be rather more hesitant, if that is not a contradiction in terms, than the primary and more straightforward task of storytelling, but it has to be attempted all the same.

One way of doing so is to develop further the group preparation of sermons (see page 77f). The minister brings to a group the results of his preliminary work on the three scriptural passages as indicated by the lectionary. Here is an objective starting point. The choice is not entirely arbitrary, but neither is it dictated unduly by our immediate concerns. As before, the group will ask questions, clarify points of detail and explore the meaning of the Biblical material. That in itself will provide food for thought, but one of its primary objectives will be to see through the material to Jesus who provides the living picture of what God is like, how he goes about his business and what are his aims and purposes. This is the God whose presence we are out to detect and proclaim.

The Old Testament offers insight into the historical, cultural and religious milieu apart from which Jesus cannot be understood. It also drops rather broad hints about matters which Jesus did a lot to clarify. The New Testament, whether dealing with doctrine or ethics or questions of the day, is everywhere a response to his life so that we ask what it was about him which made them talk as they did? The Gospels are the nearest we have to a portrait though admittedly it is open to more than one interpretation. In a sense it is not a portrait but a collection of brilliant and detailed cameos. Rather than a written testimonial describing someone's character in broad and general terms, here is a series of anecdotes based on typical incidents in his life; but added together the particular details leave the impression of a consistent though not necessarily predictable personality of such stature that many have been inclined to agree with John that if you have seen Jesus you have seen the Father.

So the group will piece together the all-important identikit picture. But in addition to this kind of discussion, centred on the Story book, it will put the Bible down for a time and talk about more

106

everyday affairs. The conversation will have to be disciplined or it may degenerate into local gossip, superficial expressions of opinion or a string of news items from the papers. In a group of varied interests, after an initial glance at a possible agenda, one item will need to be selected for more serious and extended consideration. On most occasions it will probably select itself, though a wise group will not always narrow the field to the most attractive proposition.

No selection will be necessary if the group is one of a number in the church actually organised round the realities of life. In many cases that will require a good deal of reorganisation, and that is fair enough. The reform of the Liturgy cannot be divorced from the reform of the church. Relevant worship can only flower in a community whose roots are dug deep into the soil of the world through groups of this kind or in some other way. A group may share an active concern for civic affairs or local welfare, or youth work or community relations. Others may meet round the fact that their members do a similar type of job in industry for example, or banking, hairdressing or schools. Others may meet as groups of parents or parents with children who present special problems. The possible list is endless, and the short list will be dictated by local circumstances. Some of these groups will meet for a limited period of time, others will be of an ongoing nature where people can find support and reflect together on what they are doing in the world before returning to it again with new resources and a little more understanding.

These groups may be preparing the liturgical sermon for their own act of worship. In fact the sermon may be a brief summary of some of the most important points that have emerged from an evening's talk, when, before the group disperses, bread is broken. Alternatively a group may be taking its turn at preparing the sermon for the Liturgy at which all the groups join together like cells in the body of Christ. Either way the topic of conversation will naturally be that particular area of responsibility which brings it together.

There is then a discussion about the Biblical material and a second discussion about everyday affairs, one looking at the clearest hints we have got about God and his Christlike activity, the other looking at the world in which we believe he is still at work. There are no rigid rules of procedure. The two discussions may get mixed up, though initially it is important that neither should be unduly influenced by the other so that they relate rather too conveniently. Eventually one certainly hopes that they will be related, and most groups that talk hard and go deep uncover thought provoking links or experience moments of insight when the penny drops and they see a connection or correspondence. How the two discussions are in fact related to one another in any carefully thought out way is a complicated subject which we cannot pursue. Like a piece of detective work it will involve looking closely at the evidence on the ground whilst bearing in mind the identikit picture which gives a good idea of what we are looking for. It will make use of well-tried methods of investigation which have proved themselves over a long period of time, and of information that has come to its notice from many different quarters. Added to this will be large doses of intuition and common sense, a measure of esprit de corps and, many suspect, the guiding though unobtrusive hand of a very senior colleague!

The exact nature of the relationship and technically correct proceedings are however of less importance than the business of constantly superimposing the Story's picture on our drawings of contemporary life and seeing the two together, in the belief that there is a fundamental continuity, even similarity, between them because they represent the same world and the same God.

The liturgical sermon then arises out of what can be said about God's way in the world in the light of these two discussions. However it may be prepared, it not only deals with the events concerning Jesus of Nazareth but, believing them to reveal a God who is still at work, it calls attention to all that appears to share in his creative suffering and invites us to look and see what is happening. Such positive proclamation, confident without being dogmatic and never afraid of a question mark, points the congregation to its Lord and, by implication, points it back to the world and to its own responsibilities for action. For if we are committed to the Story and its account of the way things are in the world, we are committed to cooperate with what we understand to be going on, rather than frustrating it. The vision is of a Christlike presence. Our poor eyesight can only discern it here and there even when worship has brought many things into focus. But we must be true to what we have discerned. To come across his tracks is to find our own sense of direction and so forge an essential link between the church's liturgical action and its missionary activity.

So far we have advanced two reasons for advocating yet another rule of thumb: "Let life invade the Liturgy". First, if the Story we tell at the Liturgy is as significant as we say it is for our lives, then it makes nonsense to separate the two. Second, and here we enter the area of changeable theological opinion, we believe that the God of whom the Story tells is a God who reveals himself as Christlike from the inside of the world and who is encountered not by turning away from our worldly affairs but by dealing with them very seriously indeed.

The preparation and preaching of the liturgical sermon is likely to be the context in which we make the most self-conscious attempts to interrelate the Story with our own contemporary stories. For the rest we shall rarely do better than juxtapose the two, and that is probably good enough. Central to the Liturgy will remain the readings, the proclamation and the four actions, with their objective concentration on the birth and ministry, death and Resurrection of Jesus. Around this will gather a pastiche of words, activities and images evoking the world about us. The resulting interplay and association of ideas, and the invitation to see two things at once, will have considerable potential for moments of vision and contribute to a less dramatic but equally important growth in awareness.

Genuinely corporate worship will probably do as much as anything else to ensure that life invades the Liturgy. The word 'genuine' should be underlined. It would be fatal if worship fell solely into the hands of the people who happened to like planning services and generally taking part in religious pursuits whilst those not so inclined were left to deal with the outside jobs and the church's responsibilities in the world. There are necessary divisions of labour, but that should not become one of them. If however there is genuine participation in the preparation and performance of the Liturgy it will be hard to keep out the realities of life, although it may take time to break down the habit of mind which for so long has kept the two in separate compartments. Where everyone contributes it is less likely that the Liturgy will become the preserve of sectional interests, above all the interest of the ecclesiastical professionals. It is not true that ministers and clergy know nothing about life 'as it really is', but it is true that, like most people, their experience is limited. If the Liturgy is solely their responsibility it will inevitably reflect their concerns. Where it is everybody's responsibility it is much more likely to be in touch with the general run of life. Ways of joining in then also become ways in which life can make its presence felt.

Prayers are an obvious area for the invasion. There is much to be said for written prayers, well prepared and available for corporate use. We should also plunder the riches of the Christian tradition and make other people's prayers our own. But the arrangements must always contain an element of flexibility to make room for what is on people's minds at the time. This could take the form of additional biddings and opportunities for brief extempore contributions so that topics of the moment can get a word in edgeways. Some prayers need to be specific if they are to be really in touch. There will be no time for a lot of detail and a good deal will have to be left out. Such limitations are themselves typical of life, though highly selective prayers can always be balanced by prayers of a more inclusive nature. To pray for the sick in general however needs to be brought down to earth by mentioning one or two cases in particular.

There are many different types of prayer, including confession, thanksgiving, dedication and adoration, but perhaps above all the prayers of intercession should be occasions when we clearly deal with the concrete realities of life. The logical and traditional place for them is after the proclamation when, having seen again what God is doing we turn our attention to the business of co-operating with him.

If we understand God to be constantly involved in our affairs in a Christlike way, prayers of intercession will not be regarded as efforts to get him moving on our behalf. He is moving already! Without expecting him to change his mind in any crude sense, we may dare to assume he will take notice of our point of view; but in the main to pray will be to open our own minds to him in the attempt to see things as he sees them and act accordingly in terms of a particular set of circumstances. We shall align ourselves with God's creative activity, envisaging what practical action we might take but believing that our genuine concern, and there is no prayer without it, can also work with his in less tangible ways.

For much of the time in the Liturgy intercessions will appear to be a brief and formal affair. We cannot expect to have adequate time for the careful reflection that intercession requires. There may be limited opportunities for the exchange of news and views in groups (see page 75 f) but in general these intercessions can rarely amount to much more than a compression and focusing of the kind of concern for others that is part and parcel of life. On informal occasions, where the Liturgy may take a more leisurely course, prayer will sound for all the world like a serious discussion about what to do next. The issue may involve the whole group or at times the group may think through the problems and opportunities of one of its members. Amidst all the talk it will not be afraid of silence, and a valiant attempt will always be made to arrive at a disciplined conclusion. Agreement will not always be reached, but the aim should be a common mind. Decisions will not always be taken, but where they are never taken serious discussion may be in danger of turning into self-indulgent chat.

We have already referred to the Pax or kiss of peace. It could represent a most striking and uncomfortable invasion of life—a jolt into the real world, as reflected in these lines from a poem by Joan Brocklesby:

> I shall not go to Church again
> They gave the peace, you see.
> My neighbour put his hands on mine
> And spoke to me.
> I do not care for that.

We are invited not merely to talk about reconciliation and the personal relationships which make sense or nonsense of everything else, but to do something about them within the Liturgical action. If the congregation is a real community and has a good deal to do with one another outside of worship it will know all about the inevitable problems of getting on with other people! This could make the Pax a particularly realistic affair, especially if it provides opportunities for unobtrusive but reconciling encounters between those concerned. It should however have a wider reference. There are other human relationships to be worked out, and not all of them are so cosy or face to face. A handshake, an exchange of words, a smile which breaks the ice may be adequate in a relatively intimate circle of friends. They are rather less so in the context of international affairs or industrial and community relations. Peacemaking here is of a rather different order and can involve anything from brute force to highly skilled diplomacy, and the Christian community should not be allowed to forget it.

The offering which follows the peace has been the object of a good deal of attention in recent years. We can make too much of it as well as too little. In earlier days it was largely made up of gifts in kind and looked like a harvest festival on every Sunday of the year. Out of it came sufficient food and drink for the meal to follow and the rest was shared with the poor. At its simplest the offering had to do with setting the table, though the fact that it got mixed up with the distribution of food parcels suggests that nobody felt the communion service could mean very much if people were allowed to go hungry. Paul probably underlines the point in 1 Corinthians 11.17–34. Greedy people who eat too much, leaving others to go without, and then proceed to share in the Lord's Supper, fail to discern the Body. They fail to understand what the Body of Christ, the Christian community, is all about, and that its members belong to each other.

At a different level the Christian tradition has found the offering an appropriate moment in the Liturgy to offer our "very selves to him: a living sacrifice, dedicated and fit for his acceptance, the worship offered by mind and heart" (Romans 12.1). To put it in less exalted terms, we are prepared to stand up and be counted. But this is no 'spiritual' act of commitment divorced from all the rest of life. Bread and wine are very much in evidence and, with them, all they have come to represent.

They are without doubt the gifts of God, but on reflection they are also the result of man getting to work on raw material: sowing and harvesting, manufacturing, distributing, financing, buying and selling, not only to meet his basic needs but to gladden his heart into the bargain. A tiny microcosm of our common life is carried in when members of the congregation move from their places and advance down the aisle with a loaf and a bottle of wine. Here is a very significant invasion, though all too often it has passed without notice. Probably nothing very elaborate needs to be done to put matters right, though it will be salutory if from time to time people carry other symbols of their life and work to the table to make clear what is always hidden under bread and wine.

What is really needed is that we should understand what we are doing and that this understanding should where possible be clearly expressed in the action. At the offering we not only declare ourselves but our intention to bring as much of life as we can into the light of these revealing events concerning Jesus of Nazareth, so that in all of it we may discover the activity of a Christlike God and co-operate with him. The bread and wine which later in the Liturgy are said to be the body and blood of Christ, confront us very forcibly with a down-to-earth God, associated with the familiar stuff of the world. We are also confronted with the startling suggestion that what looks like unpromising material is capable of being made rather more of than we imagined. The shadows are there. Creation is not to be had on the cheap. The bread will be broken, but united with Christ it seems destined to share in his Resurrection glory.

Such are the taller stories of faith, but at least when the offering is properly understood, the Liturgy is very much in touch with life. The bread and wine have a particular reference (see page 25f) but they are also representatives of what goes on in the world and, incidentally, they are more likely to be seen as such if they are not special orders purchased from ecclesiastical grocers but ordinary loaves baked at home or bought at the bread shop, and straightforward bottles of wine from the off-licence or the store down the road.

Matters of dress deserve a mention but need not detain us long, though the question about what to wear is not altogether easy to decide. Special clerical costumes, or at least the ones we usually see, can be criticised on two grounds. In the first place some of them originated as marks of rank. For example the long strip of material called a stole goes back to the scarf worn by Roman officials as a status symbol. Given our renewed understanding of the minister as a member of the laity or the people of God, we shall be wary of such distinctions. The second ground of criticism has more to do with the point now under discussion. Whether we are talking about the vestments worn by Orthodox, Roman and Anglican priests or the cassock, gown and white bands worn by some Free Church ministers, they are all alike in being old fashioned. Originally they were the everyday clothes of the time. The white bands for example are all that remains of a white neckerchief tied at the throat with the two loose ends hanging down. When fashions changed, the clergy kept on wearing what everyone else regarded as dated. The result is a minor way in which the Liturgy has grown out of touch with life.

Many would argue in favour of these clerical costumes. Like national dress, they are a valued link with the past. Others would prefer more ordinary clothes, though ordinariness should not exclude the possibility of giving the Liturgy the sense of occasion it deserves. From time to time, above all at the great festivals, it is appropriate to dress up to the nines. There are plenty of alternatives to mediaeval fancy dress, conventional best suits or best hats and coats. Nor need dressing up be restricted to the clergy, though we may wish to give the president an additional badge or robe of office if not a mark of rank. A motley and colourful assortment of clothes and styles may turn up, rather than any regiment in uniform, and dress would not be ordinary by being drab or everyday. It would be ordinary by being what people normally change into to go out for a special occasion.

The need for contemporary hymns and songs echoing the sights and sounds of our own generation, is widely recognised and increasingly met. One other suggestion, which has found some supporters, might be made in conclusion, and that is the development of

113

a secular calendar. Again it is not a completely new idea. Once the church came to terms with the fact that the world was not coming to an end but was likely to be with us for a considerable time, she began to take more notice of the passing of the days by making room in the Liturgy for the propers—those parts of the service which vary according to season. They were a constant reminder in worship of the fact that life went on, though the main influence was probably in the other direction as secular occasions became associated with the round of the Christian Year and its own seasons of Advent, Epiphany, Lent, Easter, Pentecost and the long hot summer of Trinity.

More recently worship in some denominations has been plagued by special Sundays making up a different kind of calendar altogether. It has been rightly criticised on two grounds. In the first place its interests were almost wholly ecclesiastical and included Bible Sundays, Missionary Sundays, Church and Sunday School Anniversaries not to mention the red letter days of men's, women's and young people's organisations. In the second place it tended to focus attention on various causes, some more worthy than others, and distract attention away from the central concern of the Liturgy. The informative address which frequently replaced the proclamation of the Gospel was largely made up of the kind of material which ought to have been dealt with at the intercessions.

A secular calendar should avoid these failings but would not replace the observance of the Christian Year. Set alongside, it would provide yet another juxtaposition of the Story and secular life. Such a calendar, thoughtfully prepared, open to revision and without too much local flavour, would associate most Sundays with notable dates in the diary of society. The end of the financial year, the holiday season, the beginning of term, the opening of Parliament, the Law Sessions and events in the sporting world are a few that come to mind.

If in the preparation of worship it became as much of a habit to consult this calendar as to consult the lectionary, it would be one more way of ensuring that the Liturgy is invaded with life. It would also provide a useful safeguard in at least two other respects. First it would counterbalance the inevitable narrowing of horizons which will accompany the concern that worship should be rooted in our actual commitments. Since we cannot be committed to everything our interests will be limited. This is acceptable as long as the calendar reminds us of the wider world and encourages us to relate it to our own. Second, it will be a counterbalance to our natural tendency to focus attention on the affairs of the moment. What happens to be news should not lead us to ignore what may never hit the headlines. A secular calendar would help to promote a catholic taste for the secular in the same way as the lectionary promotes a catholic taste for Biblical passages and the Christian Year a catholic taste for all the events concerning Jesus.

The determination to bring worship down to earth may affect its setting as well as its content. We may not always wish to be surrounded by traceried windows, ecclesiastical stone, brass memorial plaques and the like. One can imagine a very different environment. Plainer walls or movable screens surround the space for the Liturgy, decorated with the colours of celebration, the symbols of faith and silent witnesses to the communion of saints. But still more are covered with pictures, posters and photographs culled from the world of today like some contemporary iconostasis. Such a setting, with a Bible in the centre and a table adorned by lights and later set with bread and wine, would speak volumes about a concern for relevance. The Story remains at the heart of the Liturgy, but surrounded by such a collage of reminders, it is visibly in touch with life and, hopefully, reflects the mind of the actors who come to perform the play.

So much for allowing life to invade the Liturgy, but perhaps a more creative move is to agree to a more radical change of scenery and take the Liturgy out into life. If irrelevance, in the sense of being out of touch, can be traced to theological ideas about God's relation to the world, it can also be traced to social changes which in the long run may have had an even greater effect.

We cannot describe them here apart from reminding ourselves of one or two familiar points. Centuries ago the parish or 'district' was a sensible response in terms of organisation to the task of ministry and mission. It was usually coterminous with a village or township and served as a unit of local government. For both church and society it was recognisable as an area within which most people spent most of their time. Here they had their homes, grew up and died, worked and relaxed and played their part as members of a community. It was all on a human scale and fairly self-contained. The parish church, often visibly in the centre, was also literally in the centre of what went on and easily in touch with all the varied aspects of life.

With the industrial revolution the vast majority of the population moved into the new urban areas where everything was on a much larger scale. In order to make things manageable for the church these areas were divided up and a lot of new parishes created. Their boundaries no longer corresponded to the boundaries of people's lives. They did not contain the whole but only a part, and that has become increasingly true ever since.

Life no longer revolves entirely round the neighbourhood where people have their homes. Most of them work elsewhere in the city. Domestic and industrial affairs belong to two different worlds. Even the children may have to travel some distance for their education. Leisure pursuits and voluntary activities, involvement in civic affairs or night school can all take people a good way from home. The week-end cottage or caravan take the more prosperous even further. The life of the city and the lives of its citizens are not confined to one place. People live in many places at once and find that several communities and several localities loom large in their everyday existence.

Whereas people go out and about, the church tends to stay in the residential neighbourhood. Our 'local' or parish church is never thought of as being in the locality where we work but is automatically assumed to be a church nearer home where it is closely in touch with some parts of life and out of touch with many others. It is not surprising that it associates more easily with family life and finds great difficulty in relating realistically to industrial, commercial and political affairs beyond exhorting the faithful on Sunday to be good Christians on Monday. It is not easy to be effective at arm's length. Nor is it any real solution to invite the faithful to bring the affairs of the shop floor and the city centre into the life of the so-called 'local' church. A considerable distance lies between the suburban semi-detached and the shop floor or the city centre, and the distance is not merely geographical. At the week-ends, when we normally go to the Liturgy, people want a rest from all their other business and in many ways it is right that they should.

There is no denying the importance of the Christian congregation in the residential neighbourhood, but should it have the sole right to be called a 'local' church or be expected to minister effectively to all the localities or aspects of life in a modern city? Does not the church need to be diversified and take shape in less familiar surroundings and do not most Christians need to belong to at least two congregations or 'local' churches—home and away?

Once again the reform of worship cannot be dealt with in isolation from the reform of the church. But if the neighbourhood or suburban church is not in a position to minister to the whole of life, by the same argument there are severe limits to the amount of life that can or even ought to be brought into its Liturgy. The alternative suggests a final rule of thumb: "Take the Liturgy into Life". Let the resident company become travelling players and act out their drama on any temporary or makeshift stage they can build or occupy, so that the Story is read and proclaimed, grace is said, bread is offered and broken and shared in all the major localities of the city's life.

Those who know about these localities from the inside may well object to such a counter-invasion. It is not only impracticable but undesirable. As educationalists, industrialists, shop floor and management, administrators or business people we are paid to work not to hold services, to make bread not to break it, and holy huddles are to be avoided like the plague. They separate men from their colleagues in the worst possible way. These objections are sound though we forget that they retain much of their force in the locality of the home and neighbourhood. It is just as true there as at work that holding services is not our only responsibility, and when we do hold them we need to be equally discreet.

Quite apart from matters of principle however there are plenty of practical difficulties. A Liturgy at work and not at leisure, away and not at home, of the mid-week and not the week-end, in makeshift surroundings and not custom-built premises, cannot be the same as before. Time and circumstances will not allow it. It must remain true to the basic structure of Word and Sacrament, but after that many of our preconceived ideas as to how it is done and how long it takes to do it will have to go. Advice about alternatives will not come well from the sidelines. What is possible can only be discovered by those on the spot and even they will have to play it by ear and not according to the book.

Many have begun the adventure already. Some have been on their way for a considerable time, overcoming the isolation of the Liturgy by carrying it back into the 'factories' of life. In the nature of the case what they have done cannot be regarded as a blue-print for everybody else. What is appropriate is largely dictated by circumstances. What is clear in each case is that the locality of the Liturgy and of the Christian community which meets to do it together has changed. One thinks of a university where over twenty 'work-a-day eucharists' have been held in a week, regularly attended by some two hundred people. Most of them are closely related to work situations and take place during the natural breaks of the working day in laboratories, common rooms and lecture rooms. Although there is always opportunity for discussion, the form of service used is often no more unconventional than Anglican Series Two or Series Three.

Clearly the value of such small group activity is not wholly due to its location, but as one of a number of significant features, it proved itself creative.

Even more impressive perhaps is a story like that of Horst Symanowski as told by Robert Starbuck and by Symanowski himself in *The Christian Witness in an Industrial Society* (published by Collins in 1966). Symanowski was sent to work in an industrial region on the Rhine where the factories were full of people and the churches were large and empty. Taking a job as a labourer, over a period of five years he got to know the realities of industrial life from its language and customs to its problems and possibilities. He developed a widening circle of friends. He did not talk to them about the world of the church. He talked about their world believing that it was there or nowhere that the local church must exist for them, and that it was in terms of the ordinary conversations of their working lives that the Word of the Gospel must become flesh.

Symanowski's work-mates would never come to the local parish church with him on Sundays. They did enjoy discussing the text of his sermon and helping him to argue out what he should say. Gradually as confidence grew their own indigenous church began to take shape and along with it the Liturgy. Two rather different sets of arrangements are mentioned. A hostel-cum-community centre had been built under Symanowski's leadership for the use of industrial workers and others. They did not wish to come to regular Sunday services. They preferred to spend the time elsewhere with their families after being at the factory all week. But every six weeks they brought their families to the centre for 'Gossner Sunday', so named after the centre. There would be lively discussion for over an hour. Based on a biblical text or theme it never strayed far from reality. It was followed by prayers, the Lord's Supper, a midday meal round the same tables and afterwards coffee and more discussion. Here was the service of Word and Sacrament deep within the work environment.

It was to go deeper when arrangements were made for Gossner's night life! The shift workers could never take part in evening activities like other people. They were either at work, getting ready for work, or asleep. The best time for them to meet turned out to be from eleven at night until two in the morning, and this was done. For the most part it was a social occasion over a drink, but again there were conversations, meals were shared and bread was broken. The Liturgy had been taken back into life.

Similar moves have proved their worth even in the more traditional residential localities where church buildings have come to signify a God apart from the everyday, and worship has remained stubbornly remote. It has returned to life by being removed from its religious setting and, in primitive style, done once again in the house. Here the story is more familiar and is told in classic manner in what Ernest Southcott actually did in Halton, Leeds and then wrote about in *The Parish Comes Alive* (published by Mowbray in 1956).

In the end it may not be the imaginative ideas that are most required, filling out the Liturgy with numerous aids to relevance, evoking the sights and sounds of ordinary experience. A comparatively traditional Liturgy, plain and simple but set in an ordinary place amongst ordinary things and done as things are usually done, may do more than anything else to bring this extraordinary Story into touch with our lives, creating for us visions of a Christlike God active in a many-splendoured world and provoking us to wonder and celebration.

INDEX

Most of the subjects listed are dealt with in *A Dictionary of Liturgy and Worship* edited by J. G. Davies and published by the S.C.M. Press. Many of the articles include suggestions for further reading.